My Divine Comedy
A Mother's Homeschooling Journey

by Missy Andrews

CENTER FOR LIT
CenterForLit Press | Rice, Washington

Copyright © 2020 Center For Lit, Inc. First Edition.
ISBN-13: 978-0-9983229-7-1

No part of this book may be reproduced, transmitted, photocopied, or recorded without permission in writing from the publisher.

Published by CenterForLit Press, a division of
The Center for Literary Education
3350 Beck Road, Rice, WA 99167
www.centerforlit.com

Cover art by Megan Andrews

Acknowledgments

No project happens in a vacuum, and this work is no exception. This memoir would not have come to be without a few important people:

I thank my husband, who is my reader, my sounding board, my encourager, my true North, my love, and my best friend. Your love and faith have borne me up throughout the circumstances I relate within this narrative. Likewise, your vision for this project has sustained my own.

I thank my kids, who endured my years of maturation, who suffered with me, who forgave me, and who will, undoubtedly, see me in the mirror someday when they discover themselves in the leading role of their own idolatry dramas. May you find grace sufficient when you do and know that you remain beloved.

I thank my mother, Carolyn Wiles, who read several versions of this manuscript, offering suggestions and edits, as well as the encouragement necessary to soldier on. You were the first witness of God's love to me, and your constant support and prayer have given me confidence to write. I thank my father-in-law and mother-in-law, Robert and Jill Andrews, who likewise read, edited, and cheered, witnesses to this birth as you were to the births of your other "grandchildren." Your teaching, your transparency, and your forgiveness have taught me the gospel. I am blessed to have been grafted into your family.

To my friends, Wendy Johnson, Kathy Panabaker, and Elisa Kruse, co-laborers in the vineyard of home education, thank you for forgiving me my idolatry and self-righteousness and continuing to call me sister.

To the staff at Mockingbird, your faithful work of applying the gospel to every area of life provided me with the necessary framework to sort through my own experiences, to discern my sin, and to discover God's grace in my circumstances.

I thank my professors, Dr. Mike Bauman and Dr. Dan Sundahl, who first confronted my mistaken idea of education. Likewise, I thank Dr. Deborah Deacon, director of the Masters program at HMU at the time of my writing, whose enthusiasm for this narrative gave me confidence that someone from "outside my tribe" might read and understand.

Table of Contents

Author's Preface 7

Introduction 13

Ideals and the Real:
Why We Homeschool 15

A Matter of Means and
Ends: My Divine Comedy 25

The Way: Gaining an
Educational Philosophy 35

Prodigals and Performers 46

Blind Guides: Identity
Confusion and the Homeschool Mom 58

The Death of Kings: Relationships
and Homeschooling 74

Mad Men and Pasteboard Masks:
Rebellious Creatures and the Hidden God 87

Better Conduct: The Performer 93

Becoming Socrates: My
Homeschool Education 104

Little Onions and New Wine:
The Banquet of the Suffering 115

Glorious Grace: The Great Game Changer 122

The Fortuante Fall: A Paradox
of Severe Mercy 132

Blind Kings, Man-Eaters, and
Getting What We Don't Deserve:
Finding Life Through Death 142

Graceful Homeschooling 158

Things I Would Tell My Younger Self 164

Afterward 174

Bibliography 177

Author's Preface
Finding My Voice: On Being Seen

I meet a lot of moms like me at the homeschool conventions I attend with my husband. I see myself in their fears, their fatigue, and their public faces. Certain there is a standard they're not meeting, they die privately over their perceived failures, suffering alone the shame and guilt implicit in their humanity. The "little-l" laws of the world judge them to death, and they find these laws everywhere: in their children's play groups, their church Bible studies, their homeschool co-ops, and their best friend's living rooms. They see them in the media, in music, in self-help books, in local whole food crazes, in the perfection of Pottery Barn catalogues, and in the college selection board that will one day decide their children's futures. The voice of the law resides in their hearts and continually tells them they are doing it wrong.

This is one reason, I believe, that they go to homeschool conventions. They know their failure, and they are looking for some guru who has it all together to throw them a bone and give them a fix, a better way to do it right. Well, I'm no guru, but I am throwing the bone here. It comes from my dead carcass, and throwing it amounts to throwing myself under the bus publicly. But hey, if I'm already dead, what can a bus do to me?

I realize that may sound accusatory, but I don't mean it as an accusation as much as a heads-up. What follows may not be what you'd expect from a homeschooling retrospective. It's not a book of lists and directives. You won't find many "to-do" items inside. Instead, you'll find a narrative memoir that chronicles the education I received through our family's homeschool project. From youthful zeal and idealism to the tempered humility brokenness works, I invite my readers into these chapters of my life.

Writing this book is an act of faith, a declaration of the gospel of grace and the effect it continues to have on my life. This is because writing for publication requires being seen and known, which would be all right if it were a foregone conclusion that being known ensured being loved, but I have lived in the world long enough to know that such love is rare. Human nature jumps on weakness like flies on honey; so, any self-conscious declaration of failure, especially one that links that failure to the ubiquitous human condition, is sure to draw criticism.

Only last night I received notification of a comment on one of my recent blog posts. When I checked it, I was perturbed to find that the commenter had not written to

Preface

discuss any of the ideas present in my post, but rather to criticize in lengthy prose my use of the comma, schooling me in grammar like my freshman English teacher. I felt like my post was bleeding red ink that somehow stained my cheeks with public shame. If a grammar critique hit me that hard, what will real criticism do to me? All this person saw was my punctuation error; what would she do with some real material – like my personal sins and failures?

In the science fiction novella *The Great Divorce*, author and theologian C.S. Lewis tells a story of purgatorial ghosts on a day-trip to heaven. Reading it, I discovered another woman like me. Approached by one of the shining, solid beings sent from the inner precincts of heaven to induce her to go "further up and further in," the woman, aware of her transparent insufficiency, replies, "Can't you understand anything? Do you really suppose I'm going out there among all those people, like this?" The dialogue between her and the shining being follows:

> *"But why not?"*
> *"I'd never have come at all if I'd known you were all going to be dressed like that."*
> *"Friend, you see I'm not dressed at all."*
> *"I didn't mean that. Do go away."*
> *"But can't you even tell me?"*
> *"If you can't understand, there'd be no good trying to explain it. How can I go out like this among a lot of people with real solid bodies? It's far worse than going*

> *out with nothing on would have been on Earth. Have everyone staring through me."*
> *"Oh, I see. But we were all a bit ghostly when we first arrived, you know. That'll wear off. Just come out and try."*
> *"But they'll see me."*
> *"What does it matter if they do?"*
> *"I'd rather die."*
> *"But you've died already. There's no good trying to go back to that."* [1]

Any person with the slightest degree of self-awareness will acknowledge that being "seen" is a terrifying proposition. The real person, the genuine article, is a mass of contradictions. He is *simul justus et peccator*, that glorious combination of saint and sinner that Reformation theologian Martin Luther so aptly characterized. Although he bears the image of God Himself, that image is marred and magnified by original sin as it finds practical expression in his life. To be "real" in public is, therefore, akin to being naked in public – worse, the ghostly woman suggests, since it means not being seen so much as being seen through. The fear of transparency is real, and my heart shares this woman's sentiments when I contemplate going to print: "I'd rather die."

The response of the solid being, however, does my heart good upon this occasion: "But you've died already. There's no good trying to go back to that." My identi-

---

1. C.S. Lewis, *The Great Divorce* (San Francisco: HarperCollins Pub., 2001), 60-61.

Preface

fication with the crucified Christ has already mortified me. What, then, could possibly be the use of such posthumous self-preservation? I have spent many years writing things that hide unread on my computer. Often, these things have contained admissions of my failed attempts to make much of myself and my kids. This private acknowledgement of my dead works, together with my silent acceptance of the living works of Christ, have certainly done me good. For that goodness to be available to others, however, I know that I need to find my voice. Consider the publication of this book the breaking of the silence and the first fruits of the resurrection Christ has worked in me. I will trust in His righteousness and give Him glory even if that means the death of my own.

I quote the well-known theologian and gadfly Robert Farrar Capon from his *Kingdom, Grace, and Judgment*: "The truth, rather, is that the crosses that will inexorably come...and the death that will inevitably result from them – are, if accepted, all we need. For Jesus came to raise the dead. He did not come to reward the rewardable, improve the improvable, or correct the correctible; he came simply to be the resurrection and the life of those who will take their stand on a death he can use instead of on a life he cannot."[2] So, I speak – in a wavering, but audible voice. I pray that the Lord would honor this feeble proclamation of my own death, seeing

---

2. Robert Farrar Capon, *Kingdom, Grace, Judgment: Paradox, Outrage, and Vindication in the Parables of Jesus* (Grand Rapids: Eerdmans, 2002), 317.

in it that mustard seed of faith Jesus invoked. May He magnify it to proclaim with deafening intonation the present power of the risen Christ for those who are weary of self-preservation, self-promotion, and self-salvation projects. May He magnify His life in our dead bones and bring about the fruitfulness of the kingdom in our lives and families.

Missy Andrews
November 2019

Introduction
A Brief Word of Explanation

Art has an amazing ability to draw people together. Each art object, though uniquely itself and unlike others, works with the common matter of man and so participates in a tradition much larger than itself. Thus, a particular artistic piece, without losing its individuality, bears witness to a corporate or universal human experience. It is upon this principle that I reference the great books in this memoir. The works I have quoted are intended to serve as witnesses to the commonality of my own experience. I cite them to illustrate and to support my thoughts and experiences and to place myself within a larger community. To treat sufficiently the novels themselves is beyond the scope of this project. Of course, my comments do assert particular readings of these stories and so in this way may be seen as a casual participation in the literary conversation about them.

These stories were instrumental in equipping me to voice what might have otherwise remained only inarticulate rumblings in my belly. For this reason, I am deeply indebted to their authors. Their art has offered me points of light in what might otherwise have been a long, dark night of the soul. Their voices spoke to me in what might have been, without them, a kind of prolonged solitary confinement. Instead their artistic efforts drew my recognition, fostered my understanding, and fitted me within a historic, cross-cultural community. As Lewis says of the natural friendship that grows between men of common interest, these authors had me saying, "What, you too? I thought I was the only one!" Their works have convinced me that the particular experiences I relate in this book, though biographical, are not peculiar to me or even to homeschoolers, but are truly and universally human.

Isn't this the beauty of art? It provides a touchstone in the human drama. It says, as Virginia Woolf voices through her character Lily Briscoe in her poetic novel, *To the Lighthouse*, "Life stand still here." Like Lily, I've tried to make sense of my own narrative, to draw the pieces of my disparate and mystifying experience together with a line. So have countless other artists and thinkers, whose works we have as testimony to such efforts. We are surrounded by this great cloud of witnesses. The words of these artists have heartened me. They have given me caution and comfort. They have offered me fellowship in my suffering and made me wiser. It is my prayer that this work might function similarly in some small way for my readers.

Chapter 1

Ideals and the Real: Why We Homeschool

> "'You said, "everything was lawful," and how frightened you are now,' Smerdyakov muttered in surprise."[1]
>
> "...[W]hat's the good of believing against your will? Besides, proofs are no help to believing, especially material proofs."[2]

Adam and I had been engaged for only three months, and we were already arguing about how we would raise our children. Never mind that they had yet to be conceived! The issue was education, and he was determined that we would homeschool. Not only did I attend public school, but my parents were public school teachers. I

---

1. Fyodor Dostoevsky, *The Brothers Karamazov* in *The Great Books of the Western World Vol. 48*, ed. Mortimer J. Adler et al. (Chicago: Encyclopaedia Britannica, 1990), 347.
2. Dostoevsky, *The Brothers Karamazov*, 353.

argued obstinately that if public education was good enough for me, it would be good enough for my kids. I don't remember how this argument ended at the time, but I do know that when our eldest son was only two years old, I came to bed one night with an article about popular approaches to homeschooling. I remember that Adam remarked with some surprise, "So I guess we're homeschooling then?" Without even a blush, I replied in the emphatic affirmative: Of course we were homeschooling! Whatever gave him the idea that we would do anything else?

What changed during those few, intervening years? To my recollection, we never discussed the issue of education again after that initial argument; yet, I had become as decided in my heart as he that homeschooling was the only option for us. Over the years, I've thought a great deal about my change of heart and have arrived at some ideas about what may have caused it.

Before our first child was born, our children were more an idea than a reality. It was easy enough then to talk about the philosophical reasons to do one thing or another with them. Renowned atheist Ivan Karamazov, a character from nineteenth-century Russian novelist Fyodor Dostoevsky's *The Brothers Karamazov*, would have related. He argued that, in a world without God, everything is lawful. That is, he argued this until his half-brother Smerdyakov believed him and murdered their despicable father. Then, Ivan could not disguise his horror: "You said, 'Everything was lawful,' and how frightened you are now," Smerdyakov chided. Where logical proofs failed to convince Ivan of a higher law, his personal experience succeeded. When the devil himself mysteriously appeared to Ivan one evening, he too affirmed this: "…what's the good of believing against your will? Besides, proofs are no help to believing, especially material proofs." Even the enemy knows that the mind believes what the heart has chosen. Yet although Ivan prefers his idea of a material universe to a supernatural one, his conscience testifies experientially to the contrary.

Just as Ivan's ideology ran into his reality, so did my ideas about education and parenting collide with my practical experience, and despite my belief in God, I hear a lot of Ivan in my old argument with my husband. I talked about the future education of my theoretical children as though my own ideas would determine reality for them and for me. When our oldest son was born, however, I discovered viscerally that a reality exists apart from my ideas. God is, and because He created this world, it runs according to His ideas, not mine. Things just are what they are. Motherhood is what it is. No matter how emphatically I wished to believe that public school would be "good enough" for my hypothetical children, my experience with my real child proved a different matter. My two-year-old son, looking up at me with absolute trust, was no idea. He was a reality, and there was no way I was going to put him on a school bus to spend eight hours a day being introduced to the stuff of life by strangers, who, regardless of their good intentions, could never love him as I did. The thought never crossed my mind.

We would homeschool. It was decided. The only question that remained was how? With which curriculum and method would we embark on the daunting task of educating our precious charge? I pored over pamphlets, read countless books on the subject, and finally settled upon the classical paradigm, reasoning that any methodology that had survived since the time of the ancient Greeks must be good!

Some homeschooling friends in our local church were great resources for me when I was just getting started. They had organized a homeschool co-op which met once a week for group classes. One of the mothers taught German in her living room to twenty or so homeschooled kids. I looked on with fascination. The process of education I witnessed was organic, just an extension of their family and church life. The children's days were not subdivided into various "worlds"; consequently, a unity of identity was established before they had even gained self-awareness.

Learning, too, was organic rather than contrived. It was not an activity that took place in an institution or a work of magic conjured by professionals. Education was happening everywhere: in the grocery store, at the

Ideals and the Real

kitchen counter, during lap time and read-alouds, while the children played, colored, and sang. For these kids, learning was life, and life occurred within the family.

I noticed, too, that although these families approached education from a variety of different perspectives, their children were learning, and learning quickly. Most were precocious. The few that were slower never suspected it. They were a part of the family, and as such, they were accepted as they were, never labeled. Learning challenges were seen as just that–challenges–and their parents faced those challenges with them, teaching them that they were not alone. They were not losers or outsiders; they were beloved members of their family. They belonged.

This is what I wanted for my children. The security and confidence that these kids exuded were like nothing I had ever seen or experienced, and I was willing to lay down my life to provide it for my own kids. Self-sacrifice really resonated with me. I was young and eager to do something significant with my life. Educating my children would be that something.

It's an understatement to say that I embarked on homeschooling wholeheartedly. I threw myself into the project as only a type-A person could. By the time Ian was four years old, I had already attempted formal lessons. I remember his first day of homeschool. When Adam came home from work, he asked Ian about it: "Son, you had your first day of school! What did you learn?" Little, loquacious Ian piped up, "I learned: Sit still! Pay attention!" Had Adam asked that question of me, my response would have been a bit different. I had learned that you can't teach a four-year-old his numbers, letters, colors, and shapes all in a single morning! I had also learned that this homeschooling thing was a little more difficult than it looked.

In my second attempt, I tried modeling the alphabet in clay to utilize the various "learning pathways" I had read so much about. As I shaped the letter "s," I made its sibilant sound and likened it to a coiled snake, springing from the table. I guess I thought that simulating the snake's movement would cement the sound into Ian's memory. It cemented it all right; it scared him to death! That lesson devolved into tears – his and mine. Needless to say, my early efforts at teaching were fraught with failure and loaded with expectations, both for Ian and for me.

In and among the failures, of course, we experienced some successes, but these tended to happen when I wasn't looking. I recall the day Ian learned to read. He had resisted phonics and despised his reading lessons. As the oldest of six kids, he was the first to begin school and thought it completely unfair that he had to stop playing and sound out letters while his siblings continued their games without him. Not only that, but, as I later learned, he hated to fail as much as I do; he was afraid to make mistakes. Consequently, our phonics lessons were like tug-of-wars. He tugged against my desire for him to learn, and I tugged against his desire to play. About a month before my fifth child was born, I decided to shelve his lessons until after the birth. Christmas

Ideals and the Real

loomed large, and my ankles were bulging from the excess weight I was carrying. School could wait, and it did.

When Ian and I returned to our lessons in January, he opened his reader and read a complete sentence without a single mistake. The joy that lit his face when he realized what he had done was ample reward for previous weeks of frustration. He leapt to his feet and did a happy dance crying, "Mama, I can read!"

And read he did. From that day forward, I found it difficult to keep him in books. He read voraciously, feeding his verbal little mind with a feast of vocabulary and his soul with all manner of transcendent truths.

Since my degree was in literature, finding new books for him was one of my favorite tasks. I combed through used bookstores, building a home library that rivaled the children's section of our town's public one. I became familiar with authors and developed favorites. I created booklists and more booklists. I became the book lady. Short on shelf space, I piled books in corners and used them for coffee tables. Have you ever read Sarah Stewart's picture book, *The Library*? My house looked a little bit like that. Every time Ian finished a book, we'd traipse downstairs to browse our shelves for a new one. "How about this one, Ian? This is one of my favorites. It's about this boy who gets a magical cupboard for his birthday that brings his toy Indian to life! Or how about this one? It's about a boy who finds a golden ticket in a chocolate bar and gets to go on a special tour of a secret candy factory." He would listen to each summary with anticipation and march off to bed with a stack of possibilities tucked under his arm.

Once Ian had been bitten by the book bug, I found my homeschooling efforts to be much easier. A culture of learning was developing in our home, and Ian's siblings were only too interested in getting involved. When I tried to postpone kindergarten a year for my third child in order to focus on his older sister, he would not be denied. He sat at our feet as we thumbed through phonogram flashcards, spouting off the sounds and rules as quickly as she did. Although he was 18 months her junior, he progressed, lockstep through school with her, keeping pace nicely and making my efforts a two-for-one special. Learning had become the stuff of life and family for us, a shared, rich experience in which we were all invested.

Sounds pretty idyllic, doesn't it? Lest this picture fade into soft focus, let me sharpen the edges a bit. If you have ever been invested in something, you have probably discovered the power the project comes to exert over you. You might have noticed how that good thing you initially committed to begins slowly and imperceptibly to control you as you pay into it with labor and tears. "Sweat equity" aptly describes the attachment that develops between person and project in such cases. The more the project costs you, the less willing you are to cash out of it.

Before too long, I was invested up to my eyeballs. I spent all of my waking hours (and some of the hours I ought to have been sleeping) planning, executing, and worrying over the education of my children. The fatigue was undeniable, the anxiety overwhelming, the loneliness pervasive, and the fear of failure debilitating. I was committed to giving my kids the best education I could, and I believed that the success of my project would somehow determine the success of their lives and my own. I labored under a cloud of practical atheism[3], strategizing and executing my work to secure my significance.

Somewhere along the way, I had conflated the issue of educating my children with the matter of success and identity. I had confused *doing* with *being*. My husband, my parents, and my friends saw my mistake. They worried about my health and happiness. I was obsessed, anxious, and exhausted. Concerned with the disproportionate intensity of my efforts and my negative self-evaluation, they reasoned with me to give myself a break, to see my successes, to be moderate. My husband suggested I scale back the class load, start the school day later and knock off earlier. My mother affirmed me with an "Award of Educational Excellence," a formal certificate from my parents "in recognition of superior instructional service" to their grandchildren. My friends offered to cover some of the many lit and language classes I taught in our co-op. I turned a deaf ear to everyone. I could not hear them for the loud and persistent demands of the

---

3. The term "practical atheism" describes a condition in which one asserts the orthodox tenets of the Christian faith, yet lives as if there were no God, as unexamined presuppositions and emotional impulses provoke responses and behavior patterns that do not align with the person's intellectual faith.

work which I believed would, in its completion, make me and my children successful.

Although I did not recognize the Law of God at work within these experiences, it still performed its faithful office in my life. While I was busy playing schoolmarm, the Law was at work in a similar capacity within me. "The Law," Paul explains, "is our schoolmaster to lead us to Christ" (Galatians 3:24). The Law says: Do this and live. Jesus put it this way: "Be ye perfect, even as my Father in heaven is perfect" (Matthew 5:8). Life through the Law demands nothing less than perfection, and my fearful heart intuitively felt that burden in the law-filled tasks of motherhood. My sense of personal identity, which was firmly attached to my performance, didn't stand a chance against the hard realities of personhood God has rooted in creation. In the fullness of time, my experience in the real world would challenge my idea of identity and throw me back on the genuine source of self, significance, and all things.

Chapter 2

A Matter of Means and Ends: My Divine Comedy

> "We have come to the place where I have told you you will see the wretched people who have lost the good of intellect." [1]
>
> "Foolish is he who hopes that our reason may compass the infinite course taken by One Substance in Three Persons. Be content, human race, with the quia; or if you had been able to see everything, no need was there for Mary to give birth; and you have seen desiring fruitlessly men such that their desire would have been satisfied which is given them for eternal grief: I speak of Aristotle and Plato and of many others." [2]

Once I embraced the idea of homeschooling, I began, as I mentioned, to look for an approach that would

---

1. Dante Alighieri, *The Divine Comedy*, trans. Charles S. Singleton in *The Great Books of the Western World Vol. 21*, ed. Mortimer J. Adler et al. (Chicago: Encyclopaedia Britannica, 1990), 3.
2. Dante, *The Divine Comedy*, 47.

unify my efforts and direct me to my final goal: I wanted desperately to raise intelligent, God-fearing children, who loved the truth and one another and who had the necessary tools to pursue their chosen vocation. I wanted to ensure their happiness and success so much that my own seemed inextricably attached to it.

From my perspective, that required giving them a superior education. I found an article in a magazine that succinctly laid out some approaches to homeschooing and weighed their differences. I had in mind a "final product" of homeschooling and was looking for a paradigm that would get us there. I wanted a program inspired by real academics, and by real I meant classical.

The liberal arts were my passion. I had received such an education, and as I already confessed at the outset of this narrative, what was good enough for me was, by my way of thinking, undoubtedly good enough for my children. (If you were to detect a little narcissism here, you wouldn't be wrong.) At this early point in my homeschooling career, I'm afraid that I shopped for educational approaches like I shopped for clothes. I was looking to express my personal tastes and to acquire something that would make my family look really good. (If you were to detect a hint of sarcasm here, you wouldn't be wrong.) Consequently, I pee-shawed Jim Holt's No-Schooling methodology as anti-education. I relegated Delight Directed Learning to the realm of pandering to the whims of children. I derided Better-Late-Than-Earliers as benighted left-behinders. Only classical education, in all its shiny reincarnation, smelled like the real thing to me,

A Matter of Means and Ends

and only the real thing would do for my children. Classical education had the appeal of erudite sophistication and intellectualism, not to mention staying power! This was the educational carrying card of the ancients; Socrates endorsed these methods. This was the kind of elite company I was interested in keeping, the image I was interested in cultivating for my family.

Surely, I can hear you thinking, *you didn't really think such things*. Although I certainly would not have admitted it in such terms then, I'm afraid I didn't see myself well enough to realize that I most certainly did. Of course, I loved my kids and wanted to do what was best for them. I wanted to equip them for success. I wanted a program that would teach them to use their minds, develop their abilities, and strengthen their weaknesses. I wanted to help them become good students, responsible people with vision for the world and their lives. I wanted all of these things, and classical education proved a fine paradigm toward achieving them. In a fallen world, however, in a fallen person, there are no pure motives.

The human heart is a complex thing. Even if a person wished to, it would prove difficult to divine the myriad motives that combine to move him. David laments: "Who can understand his errors? Cleanse me from secret faults" (Psalm 19:12). Human beings do things for a variety of reasons, and when we narrate those reasons to ourselves and others, we generally choose to include only the ones that present us in the best light. I know I am being hard on humanity here, but I think it is the truth. We are invested in being good guys; so, we acknowledge the good guy parts of our stories much more readily than the uglier, more self-interested parts.

So for the sake of context and transparency, a little personal history might clarify matters. I am the daughter of two teachers. I am also a habitual pleaser. An overachiever in school, I learned to seek validation through academics. Upon earning a B.A. in two majors, I married the co-valedictorian of my college class, and together we re-located to pursue graduate degrees at a university in Virginia renowned for integrating worldview and career goals.

We were a couple of Christian ideologues, Adam and I, motivated by zeal and committed to applying Christian principles to our life together. The centrality of the family in God's work of building His Kingdom dominated our understanding of Christian living. Aware of the feminist agenda to push mothers into the workplace, I self-consciously committed to be a stay-at-home mom even before we had children. I fully believed (and I still do) that the greatest work of a mother is to train up her children in the nurture and admonition of the Lord (Ephesians 6:4).

Moreover, the "full quiver" philosophy dominated our imagination and dictated our understanding of success. Extrapolated from Psalm 127:4, which compares children to weapons useful against the onslaught of the enemy of this world, this philosophy discourages the use of birth control. Performer that I was, I received this simile as a law and concluded that motherhood was the single most valuable career a woman could undertake.

A Matter of Means and Ends

By extension, I assumed that the more children a mother raised, the more significant she herself became. So, I pulled on my boots (you know, the kind with big straps) and got busy.

The stork began his regular visits to our house when I was only a month into my first semester of graduate work. I laid down my own educational goals and came home to make motherhood my full-time occupation. I found myself ill, alone most of the time, and staring my self-pronounced ideology of motherhood straight in the face.

My problem was not the actual work of homemaking. Nesting was in my blood, and, true to my type-A personality, I took to the job of creating a "well-ordered haven of domesticity" with a vengeance. The only trouble was that I was used to finding validation in my grades, and no one gave me an A for cleaning the oven or vacuuming the floors. No one cared if my drawers were well-organized or my silver polished to a sheen. Since we had only met a few people in the state of Virginia at that time, few ever saw my meticulously decorated, hand-crafted, artisanally curated abode. (Alas, Facebook was yet to come!) My heart longed for validation, and I pursued it relentlessly.

Once the aforesaid arrows began to accumulate in our quiver, we began the hard work of training them. This process involved discipline and education, which brings me to our present conversation. I faced homeschooling with all the energy I'd brought to the classroom, the home arts, and the birthing room. Every part of my being was trained to the task. I was determined to prove my mettle in my homeschooling efforts. I would make a mighty blow against the kingdom of darkness by raising and educating my children in the nurture and admonition of the Lord. They would be world changers!

I think that paints the scene pretty well. Suffice it to say that when you put two chronic performers together, even if they are well-meaning performers, you get a whole lot of arrogance. You could say that I entertained a relatively high anthropology. I believed myself capable of better things than a proper understanding of human nature really supports.

From my present vantage, the main problem was not my ideas about family or the blessing of children, nor was it my belief in the superiority of home education. The problem was the use to which I aimed to put these very good things. My best intentions were corrupted by my subconscious desire to prove myself successful and to secure my own identity.

It is easy to mistake the gift of God for the Giver and worship it instead of Him. Man's religious heart keeps him looking for something to worship, and since that heart is fallen, it often gets it wrong. The Apostle Paul observes this error in the pagan Romans, who "[p]rofessing to be wise, ...became fools and changed the glory of the incorruptible God into an image made like corruptible man – and birds and four-footed beasts and creeping things" (Romans 1:22-23). He alludes to a similar impulse in the Athenians: "Then Paul stood in the midst of the Areopagus and said: 'Men of Athens, I perceive that in all things you are very religious'" (Acts 17:22). These scriptural accounts reference man's innate inclination to worship creation instead of the Creator. This is the substance of idolatry.

In Paul's time, idols were obvious. Stone figures with shrines erected in their names peppered the Mediterranean world. These lie in ruins today. It would be a mistake to think, however, that just because modern man has put away his stone images, he has also put away idolatry. Today's idols may be more abstract and nuanced than those of the ancients, but they exert the same influence over their worshipers. Whatever we worship gains the status of an idol, be it a person, beauty, sports, success, fame, wealth, sex, happiness, education, or parenting.

The Bible is not the only book to observe man's religious leanings. Classic literature also records man's search for a god. Some seekers come nearer the mark than others. Some authors explore meaning in love. They depict the individual's quest for a romantic partner as a search for personal identity and a meaningful life. Of course, if their story reads long enough, it often ends in sorrow because people inevitably die or disappoint. Romantic love fails in the role of deity. Other authors depict men who pursue meaning through business or the arts, fame or wealth, with similar results. This is the beauty of literature: When we read about the pursuits of other men, we inevitably see ourselves. From ancient to postmodern, literature suggests that all men crave meaning and identity, and most mislocate it. The human heart is, as reformer John Calvin suggests, a perpetual factory of idols.[3]

Perhaps the author of Proverbs hits nearest the mark when it comes to describing my own idolatrous tendency: "Do not be wise in your own eyes; fear the Lord and depart from evil" (Proverbs 3:7). Intellectual arrogance is a subtle form of idolatry, a turning of the eyes from the only wise God to the self. Regardless of the vehicle, be the image stone or flesh, whatever we court more than God is an idol.[4] Human beings to a man, in their pursuit of God, are prone to love either the wrong things, or the right things in the wrong way.

Medieval author Dante Alighieri depicts this in his

---

3. John Calvin, *Institutes of the Christian Religion, 6th American Edition, Revised and Corrected, Volume 1*, trans. John Allen (Philadelphia: Presbyterian Board of Publication, 1813), 1.XI.8, http://www.gutenberg.org/files/45001/45001-h/45001-h.html.

4. Multiple theologians and church catechisms affirm this assertion. For example, Martin Luther, in his Large Catechism, states "A 'god' is the term for that to which we are to look for all good and in which we are to find refuge in all need. Therefore, to have a god is nothing else than to trust and believe in that one with your whole heart. As I have often said, it is the trust and faith of the heart alone that make both God and an idol. If your faith and trust are right, then your God is the true one. Conversely, where your trust is false and wrong, there you do not have the true God. For these two belong together, faith and God. Anything on which your heart relies and depends, I say, that is really your God" (Martin Luther, *The Large Catechism*, trans. F. Bente and W. H. T. Dau (St. Louis: Concordia Publishing House, 1921), 386, http://www.gutenberg.org/cache/epub/1722/pg1722-images.html.

epic, *The Divine Comedy*. Dante casts himself as protagonist in this drama, fighting through a mid-life crisis brought on by his futile attempts to climb the mountain to God through good behavior. Three allegorical beasts bar his way: a leopard (representative of lust), a lion (symbolic of pride), and a wolf (the image of avarice). Thwarted by his sins, the persona Dante receives help from an unexpected outside source. The ghost of his favorite poet, Virgil, materializes to guide him on an exploratory field trip through the regions of the afterlife to help him discover the true source of goodness.

In the first part of his journey, Dante descends into Hell. There he discovers the damned, those who on earth perverted love by one means or another. Mistaking the good gifts of God for the Giver, each had fallen into his own idolatry. As their earthly pursuits became their gods, they "lost the good of intellect." Reason, Virgil explains, teaches man to worship the Giver of gifts alone. The shades had worshiped the gifts instead and found themselves eternally damned to impotent knowledge of this, their unreasonable error.

Like Dante, I have been the main character in a comedy of my own. Like his shades, I too confused gifts and Giver by making motherhood and home education (good occupations both) end goals, rather than subordinate means to the greater end of "glorifying God and enjoying Him forever." Motherhood and home education were not designed to be gods, but fruitful work. "For we are his workmanship, created in Christ Jesus for good works, which God prepared beforehand, that we should walk in them" (Ephesians 2:10). When I made these good things primary, pursuing them as a source of identity and validation, I perverted them. I loved the right things, but in the wrong way.

I had not yet made Dante's ultimate discovery of the Divine Love, who Fathers all created things and gives them their proper names. Like Dante, I acknowledged God and the need to reach Him, but I was lost in my own dark wood of error and confusion. Because I had not yet learned to know myself as the passive object of God's love, I continued blindly to value the gifts as goodness itself and to confuse my identity with my function.

I looked to my activities as a mother and educator for identity, value, and acceptance. Unfortunately, anything smaller than God is too small to fill His office in our lives. Put to this service, such a thing becomes, regardless of its inherent goodness or usefulness, a demon which turns on us and devours us whole. Such is the story of my foray into motherhood and home education.

Chapter 3

The Way: Gaining an Educational Philosophy

> *"I have had moments of self-knowledge that certainly made me better, but never one that made me feel better."*[1]

As I already mentioned, my first move once I committed to home education was to find a pedagogical methodology, a good teaching philosophy. Before I made my choice, I waded through a good bit of literature, trying to get the lay of the land from various gurus of home education. Each of them claimed to have the secret recipe for raising and educating children. Their formulas made the process of homeschooling and child rearing look a lot like baking muffins. All I needed was

---

1. Richard Mitchell, *The Gift of Fire* (New York: Simon & Schuster, 1987), 71.

a good recipe, and I would get a perfect rise every time. When I looked at their families, I found all the proof I needed. They looked great! Their kids were as well-groomed, respectful, and accomplished as they. How could I lose? Not only that, but their programs looked exciting!

Their booklists looked even better, and there is little I love more than a page of well-selected titles. Booklists smell like education, and the longer and more challenging the better. Reading them, however, I realized with anxiety that, despite my literary education, I had actually read very little of what was considered the canon of Western literature. Faced with time constraints, my lit professors had used anthologies and excerpts in order to introduce me to authors and literary movements. As it turns out, an academic degree is just a teaser for the mind, an invitation to the feast of learning that awaits the lifetime student. Only no one told me this, or if they did, I failed to understand them. So, feeling like a fraud, I began feverishly reading every classic I could get my hands on in order to be worthy of my degree.

Maybe you have tried this, too. You find a booklist and pull up a chair for the duration. You struggle through tome after tome in an effort to somehow "arrive" at an education. The problem is that no two definitions of education look the same. Every booklist is different, every scholar's list of "must-reads" dictated largely by what they themselves have read and found important. Whose list is the measure? When have we read enough?

As if this problem were not sufficiently perplexing, it turns out that this Booklist Approach[2] to education is not the only educational paradigm out there. Add to it the Mastery Learning[3] paradigm, which suggests that the most significant thing a student must achieve is subject matter proficiency. Advocates of mastery learning suggest that there are lists of facts and content at every grade level that children must memorize, and that until they have, they ought not to progress. By this measure, an education is the mastery of a body of knowledge. Yet again, the content of these lists of facts varies from curriculum designer to curriculum designer. More often than not, they seem a bit arbitrary. Who is to say, for example, that by the second grade, an educated child should be capable of spouting off all the states and capitals without error? In addition, what guarantee can the mastery curriculum designer offer that, should Junior achieve such mastery, he will be amply prepared to solve the problems that he will inevitably face in his future academic career and personal life? More pertinently, if he fails to master these facts, will he be unprepared for anything more than the states and capitals test on Friday?

Today's latest educational trend aims for innovation.

---

2. Education pioneer Charlotte Mason and some classical education paradigms make the booklist primary in education. Certainly, the books we choose for our children are important, but is the completion of a particular booklist the measure of education? Is cultural literacy synonymous with education?
3. E. D. Hirsch, Jr.'s *Core Knowledge Series* is an example of this. His books gloss the curriculum content for proficiency and progress at every grade level.

Educational consultants stress the importance of raising problem solvers, critical thinkers[4] who can master any discipline. Give them a book, and they can learn anything. What is needed, they argue, are creative people who can think outside of the box. Only programs that foster critical thinking, we are told, will equip kids to compete in the marketplace of ideas. Critical thinking alone constitutes an education.

Meanwhile, other voices chime in reminding us that our children learn best when they follow their own curiosity,[5] or when their curriculum is interrelated and integrated[6], or when their learning styles are known and utilized.[7] We are encouraged to use the various learning pathways[8], to do extension projects that make things practical, to take field trips[9], to be sure that the kids are not tied to their books or their desks but have plenty of

---

4. The Critical Thinking Company does great work in this field. They describe critical thinking as the ability for students to "think for themselves, to question hypotheses, to develop alternative hypotheses, and to test those hypotheses against known facts" (criticalthinking.com).
5. Gregg Harris proposes this Delight Directed Learning in his book, *The Christian Homeschool*.
6. Consider the Unit Study approach to education, a platform utilized in KONOS Curriculum, The Weaver Curriculum, and Tapestry of Grace Curriculum.
7. Consider *Discover Your Child's Learning Style: Children Learn in Unique Ways*, by Mariaemma Willis and Victoria Kindle Hodson.
8. This is presented in a book originally intended for businessmen entitled *Learning Paths* by Jim Williams and Steve Rosenbaum.
9. Read "The Importance of Hands-on Learning," by Temple Grandin.

The Way

time for outdoor exploration and fort building.[10] One expert tells us that we need to give our kids a head-start by educating them young[11], while another argues that we do violence by pressuring them to learn too early.[12] Some of these suggestions prove to be mutually exclusive. Whose kids are inherently interested in the epics the first time through? Whose kids love to memorize biology lists or frankly just can't wait for the states and caps quiz?

In the homeschool marketplace, these conflicting voices augment their influence through branding. Rather than merely peddling pedagogical techniques, curriculum designers package their preferred methodologies and teaching aids as comprehensive approaches to child-rearing and parenting. Associating their ideas with a particular lifestyle or personality, they make shopping for curriculum less an examination of practical tools for the teacher and more like browsing for a personal style or family identity. Their beautifully constructed websites invite club-like participation and promise identity and fellowship to joiners.

As an untried homeschooler, I longed for the affir-

---

10. Charlotte Mason was a proponent of this. She encouraged "living books" and "twaddle free" education, replete with outdoor exploration reminicient of the likes of Thoreau. So, too, was Jim Holt, who invented the term "unschooling" and kicked off a new trend in home education. Waldorf or Steiner theories of education also stress this, especially in the early years.
11. The Head Start Program, created by Jule Sugarman, was a part of Pres. Lyndon B. Johnson's *Great Society Campaign* against poverty. Proponents advocate pre-school education starting at the age of three years.
12. Consider Raymond and Dorothy Moore's *Better Late Than Early*.

mation of such a group. I needed to know that others before me had "done it." The labor of home education can be isolating and lonely, and–since everything seems to be riding on doing it right–the burden that results is acute. While finding a curriculum fit is important, marketing strategies capitalize on this eternal search for a tribe. At one point, I'd have bought anything that promised the success I craved, and the products that accumulated on my bookshelves proved it. Furthermore, each curriculum investment staked a claim on my attention, expanding the demands on my time and my own growing sense of expectations. Inversely, every unopened curriculum package stood as a witness against me, declaring my failure.

Are you exhausted yet? I am. Every time I went curriculum shopping or found a new booklist, it was as though the powers that be, those who defined education, had changed all the rules. I would buy the new curriculum and start the laborious process of teaching all over again. Not only did this set me "behind schedule" in the universal race to "make it through the curriculum," but it also labeled me a failing educator. Every time my child got less than an A on his states and capitals test, I got less than an A on my home educator assessment. Every time the booklist sported titles that my child had not read, we were behind. Every time my kids failed to innovate, I felt they were doomed to failure, and I condemned myself to the outer realm right along with them.

On the other hand, every time I read a list and discovered that my child had read every title, I gave him

The Way

(and myself) a little pat on the back. We were on top of things. He was a sharp cookie. And every time he made a 100 percent on his states and caps quiz, I was convinced of our success. Education was happening; the test was visible proof! Similarly, whenever one of my kiddos came up with some interesting take on a problem or sported some new insight, I was encouraged that they would someday be a CEO with a posse of lackeys to do their bidding. No minimum wage jobs for them; their futures were secure because they were being educated!

Can you see where I am going here? I understood identity as something analogous to performance. I understood it to be self-created and self-sustained, therefore something that could be missed or lost. I assumed that part of my role as a parent was to create my child's identity, and the gravity of that role weighed like a great burden. Fear gripped my heart as I contemplated the project of homeschooling as a project in person-building. The inevitable "holes" or "gaps" in the educational process meant a denigration of their personhood, with me responsible for the defect. My own identity was entirely wrapped up in the success or failure of this project. I was looking for a program that would validate both my kids and me. Subsequently, I rode the wave of our daily homeschool events with my heart on my sleeve. Everything, I believed, was at stake in the effort.

I wish that I had understood early on that education is not a booklist, nor mastery, nor innovation. Education, although it partakes of all of these things, is an unquantifiable mystery.[13] Tests cannot insure it. Lists cannot contain it. Content cannot produce it. Success is no true barometer of it. In fact, failure is often a better indicator that true education is occurring. Education, that thing that equips our children for life in this world, familiarizes them with the way things really are. By "things," I mean human beings, nature, ethics, society, love, death, life – and themselves – all that partakes of the physical and metaphysical realities of the universe we call home.

As a result, the process of education is often confrontational. One of the first and most significant functions of education is to teach the student that he is not the center of the universe. The liberal arts are a rich field in which to cultivate this truth. He learns this when he is required to read the epic and do the desk work. He learns it from the subject content, too. Facts to support this philosophical reality are limitless and available in every discipline. Why, for example, does $1 + 1 = 2$? Who says? Why does a bear hibernate, or a woodpecker shut his eyes the split second before he makes contact with a tree? Why does the nucleus of an atom, packed tightly with unbonded protons and neutrons, hold together? Why does every civilization find patricide reprehensible and adultery immoral? Why do men, regardless of

---

13. My goal here is not to gainsay the admirable contributions of educational philosophers and curriculum designers, nor to dismiss the obvious value of some of their propositions, but rather to suggest that education is not a pedagogical method after all. The methods, when they are good, are only tools to foster education and never the stuff of education itself.

The Way

their place in time or culture, contemplate the good, the true, and the beautiful? Why do they honor valor? Why do they denigrate cowardice? Why do they value innocence and strive to protect it? Why do they worship? As students stumble into questions like these, they enter the timeless discussion of what it means to be human. Educators Robert Maynard Hutchins and Mortimer Adler termed this discussion of ideas the "Great Conversation," and great it is. Although these questions cannot save an individual's soul, they can reveal to him the limitations of his own mind in the face of the vast universe.

In my sophomore year at my liberal arts college, I attended a quarterly, compulsory interview with my academic advisor. He asked me how I was getting along and if I was enjoying my college experience. Yes, I replied, except for one thing that was troubling me. I was overwhelmed by the sheer magnitude of what there was to learn and feared that it was too great for me to master. With a gleam in his eye, my advisor mused, "My dear, I think you are getting what some might call an education."

Many years later, as I was preparing for my oldest child's freshman year in high school, I was, as you might expect, on the hunt for the perfect booklist. In the midst of my angst-ridden preparations, I received a call from an old college professor and friend, offering his help. Perfect timing, I replied. All I need is a booklist! What should a student read to prepare to sit in your class? Without skipping a beat, he replied, "Got a pencil? Four books: The Bible, anything by Augustine, Milton's *Para-*

dise Lost, and a book by Richard Mitchell called *The Gift of Fire*. Read the last one first, and everything else will make sense." Mystified, I ordered Mitchell's book and read it in one great gulp.

Education, Mitchell argues, is not a booklist, but an awakening. It is coming to know oneself and one's world. It is the discovery of what one is and is not. It is an activity by which one takes the measure of his own thoughts. In this way, it is an act of watching oneself think. This is, at once, the simplest thing and the most difficult. Mitchell says of it: "I have had moments of self-knowledge that certainly made me better, but never one that made me feel better." For true education reveals that man is not a god but a creature, not the master but the subject.

As hard as this challenge proves, this definition liberated me. It set me free from the tyranny of booklists and mastery education and gave me permission to admit what both taught me: I am not the measure of all things. I will never know it all. I will never read it all. I am a creature with both potential and limitations. Any method of education that fails to foster this discovery fails to educate.

Rather than arrogant answer-men, true education produces self-awareness and its constant companion, humility. It humanizes. The discovery of the nature of man (and by extension the nature of self) fosters compassion and empathy, the bedrock of human relationship and community. Socrates exhorted "know thyself," and true education fosters this self-knowledge.

The Way

If self-knowledge and identity are intimately related, then education is arguably a road to the discovery of identity. It is not, however, a road to the creation of an identity via success or failure, which reflect only function. To educate is not to create an identity for your child, and gaps in their knowledge are not defects of personhood.

Education leads a child out of the prison of the self so that he can see everything, including himself, as the creative work of a loving God. Education reveals the true nature of the individual as a creature. It teaches him to wonder at his capabilities and limitations and to look for the uncaused Cause who made him and all things. True education leads to the wisdom which Proverbs identifies as "the fear of the Lord." Only in this posture can we discover our true identities.

Chapter 4

Prodigals and Performers

> *"But the father said to his servants, 'Bring out the best robe and put it on him, and put a ring on his hand and sandals on his feet. And bring the fatted calf here and kill it, and let us eat and be merry; for this my son was dead and is alive again; he was lost and is found.' And they began to be merry"* (Luke 15:22-24).

When you think about it, Christianity provides some pretty insightful answers to the question of what it means to be human, and all of them point to the same awful, but liberating truth. The Bible tells us man is not perfect, not omniscient, not self-created, but instead a finite creature, who bears the likeness of God, but without His moral goodness. Solomon, who was himself not good, but wise, asserts: "For there is not a just man on earth who does good and does not sin" (Ecclesiastes 7:20). By this testimony, any claims or attempts to produce perfect people through education are misguided. Yet, if education cannot produce morally good children, then what good is it?

Some might argue that education is primarily a means to a lucrative job. Education is career training. By this definition, a technical school or a training course is as effective in fitting a person for life as the study of great books. Unfortunately, technical knowledge does not often come with the wisdom that helps a man employ it. A doctor may know very well what to do when a particular set of circumstances presents itself, but lack the wisdom to know whether or not to do it. The moral compass necessary to traverse such ground is rarely discoverable in a medical textbook. Facts alone are not enough to equip children to live in a world where daily decisions between seemingly equal goods are necessary. What is needed is an education that awakens the moral imagination, and since the time of Socrates educators have found stories most useful in this pursuit.

When the terms "moral imagination" or "educating for virtue" come up, many understand them to reference a sure method for producing "good" kids. Put them in front of the "right" books, and they'll learn to choose the good and reject the evil. Yet, in my experience, knowing what is right does not always translate into doing what is right. Again, I cite King Solomon as Exhibit A. Although declared by God to be the wisest of men, he engaged in idolatry and wickedness that ultimately provoked God's wrath, requiring the rending of the kingdom from Solomon's posterity. The Apostle Paul articulates this paradox between knowing and doing in his letter to the Romans: "For the good that I will to do, I do not do; but the evil I will not to do, that I practice" (Romans 7:19-20). Original sin pursues all men in their attempts to live rightly.

If knowing the good cannot produce goodness or ensure participation in the good, if beholding beauty cannot make one beautiful, if understanding virtue and paying mental assent to its qualities cannot make a virtuous person, then what good is it?

Socrates summarized education in two words: Know thyself. By his definition, the end of education is twofold: first that our kids would know virtue, and second that they would be wise. Proverbs puts it this way: "The fear of the Lord is the beginning of wisdom, and knowledge of the Holy One is understanding" (Proverbs 9:10). Paul articulates the goodness inherent in this sort of wisdom as he concludes his thought in Romans 7, querying, "What a wretched man I am! Who will deliver me from this body of death?" (Romans 7:24). True education familiarizes a child with the stuff of goodness, truth, and beauty in order to equip him with eyes to see his true condition, the shortfall between the ideal and the real. This self-awareness has the potential to awaken humility and prime the soul for an encounter with the sole source of goodness, God Himself. This is the goal of an education in virtue; this is the ultimate hope behind awakening the moral imagination: not the creation of good people, but the waking of the soul to its need for redemption.

More often, however, our most successful attempts to educate produce the linear opposites of humility: pride and discouragement. The successful students, whose moral imaginations are tickled, but not fully awakened, imagine themselves to be virtuous. Their own small accomplishments at meeting the perceived moral expectations lull them into believing themselves capable of self-salvation. They style themselves the "masters of their fate and the captains of their souls," to quote William Ernest Henley's *Invictus*. Their more imaginative, but perhaps less capable counterparts, however, despair when failures loom large upon their moral radar and condemn them as losers in the education game. Too often our efforts to educate produce either shameless self-promoters and arrogant performers, or their discouraged and defeated underachiever counterparts.

What are we doing wrong? Why does the child who struggles with math walk away from her lessons sure she is stupid? What makes math capable of defining her in this way? Just one of many branches of learning, what gives it the power to mark her identity? While we're at it, why is the precocious boy for whom every subject comes easily so sure he is better than the next guy? Furthermore, in view of his success, why is he so insecure?

At their root, these problems have little to do with math or intelligence. They have everything to do with the purpose to which kids are putting these things, and that is a result of the way education is being framed for them. Doing and being, in true Aristotelian fashion, are so conflated that success and failure are understood not as conditions, but identities.

    In my own household, this played out daily. When one of my children spouted the right answer to a phonogram card and the other lagged behind, the quick one assumed the title of Winner. The deliberate one left Loser. Both wore their titles as burgeoning identities. Somehow along the way, my kids imbibed the idea that who they were was tied up with their performance – in school, in sports, in life. Where did they get this idea? Well probably from me. Not that this was intentional; who screws up their kids on purpose? I was just passing on to my children what had been entrusted to me: Seek identity where you may find it. I found it in academics. You can, too.

    My confusion was not the only source of my children's misunderstanding, however. Performancism, that ideology which attaches identity to achievement, is shot through modern society. Nearly every element of our lives is based on conditionality. If you do this, then you will get that. If you don't, then you won't. We are taught from the beginning that in order to be successful, we must work hard, get good grades, garner honors and acclaim, find a high paying job, marry a good-looking person, for which thing we must be good-looking persons, which requires that we eat right, exercise, get plenty of sleep, but get up early to work hard, et cetera, et cetera. We are supposed to work and earn because wealth, we are told, is a component of all the shapes happiness takes, but we're not supposed to work too hard or we'll be guilty of workaholism. Everywhere you look you find instructions on how to "do it right": how to stay thin, stop the aging process (good luck with that!), have a better marriage, a prettier home, raise smarter children, and retire with dignity.

Everyone wants to "do it right" because, according to the law of performance, doing is being. The problem is that no one is capable. What's worse, when we divine our sense of self from how we are doing, then we step onto an uphill treadmill with a broken speed function that just keeps increasing. Though we may manage to perform in one arena, we are bound to fail in another. When we attach our identities to the laws that undergird our society's understanding of success, we set a crash course for fear and disillusionment. Many educational institutions offer a microcosm of this system.

Today, the culture encourages parents to begin the educational rat race while their children are still babes in the womb. One article reports that in major cities, competition for spots in the top pre-schools produces a 4-year waiting list.[1] Little Johnny is signed up before he draws his first breath. Students themselves are encouraged to begin preparing for college in the 6th grade.[2] Not only are they coached to keep up their grades, but also

---

1. The Bold Italic Editors, "The San Francisco Preschool Popularity Contest," *The Bold Italic* (May 28, 2014), Medium, thebolditalic.com/the-san-francisco-preschool-popularity-contest-the-bold-italic-san-francisco-9a350c64affe.
2. Jason Ma, "Why To Start Preparing For College In Sixth Grade," *Forbes* (April 1, 2012), https://www.forbes.com/sites/unicefusa/2019/10/15/unicef-urges-all-parties-to-protect-children-in-syria/#2eac37f3542e.

to prepare a file of extracurricular activities that demonstrate their well-roundedness, including after school jobs and civic or volunteer work. Pressure to present a perfect face to college admissions boards builds to an unhealthy extreme as every element of students' lives aims toward this singular goal. Teen suicide rates reflect this trend. When college applicants are rejected by the school of their choice, they nose-dive into deep depression.[3] Their world has ended. They are failures. Life no longer matters. They have missed the mark.

How does performancism affect the educational community? Well, it produces outcome-based education and its fruits: teaching to a test and a pre-occupation in the classroom with grades. When a teacher's job depends upon his students' measurable progress, class time ceases to revolve around engaging discussions and teachable moments. What does it do to community within a student body? Go to any school and you will see it: the "Cans" and the "Can'ts" divide into groups. Those who can find identity in their classes and grades. Those who can't look for it in sports, or popularity, or theater arts, and while these activities and the achievements within them are good things, pursuing them for identity has an unfortunate effect on the educational process. It stops. It stops with the smart kids, and it stops with the kids who think that they are dumb.

---

3. Scott Jaschik, "Suicide Note Calls Out Pressure on Students," *Inside Higher Ed* (February 12, 2018), https://www.insidehighered.com/admissions/article/2018/02/12/suicide-note-16-year-old-renews-debate-about-pressure-top-high-schools.

When kids look to academics to find identity, education just becomes too loaded; it backfires. In addition, a rivalry grows between the "factions" that disrupts any efforts toward community. In the race for identity, fellow runners are viewed as competitors. No longer are an individual's innate talents perceived as gifts to the community, but sources of personal identity and, by extension, threats to the identity and place of others.

Although I'd like to believe that this problem doesn't exist in home education, I know better. All parents desire success for their children. In fact, homeschool parents may have it worse than their day-school counterparts in that they feel uniquely responsible to produce this success. Home education and performancism often go hand in hand, and when this happens there is no facet of the child's life that is free from the pursuit of perfection. The beauty of home education is that it integrates learning and life. You've experienced it: every outing is a field trip, every interest an extracurricular. However, when these activities become weighted with performancism, where can our kids hide from the expectations? How are they to avoid conflating success and performance with acceptance and identity?

I saw this dynamic at work in relationships between the mothers in my homeschool co-op as well. Like me, they were eagerly pursuing identity even as they labored for and with their children. The gifted teachers in the co-op showed up those whose talents lay in other areas. The Cans were self-satisfied, and the Can'ts were defeated, envious, and depressed. Good friendships were strained every August when it was time to plan for the next academic year. Some would shine, and others would despair. Together we labored under the misconception that we were what we did. Interestingly enough, we teaching moms were in desperate need of education ourselves, and our mutual struggle was working to that effect even through our sinful misunderstanding.

We were like the older and younger brothers in the Parable of the Prodigal Son.[4] You remember the story: The younger brother goes to his father and says, in effect, "I wish you were dead. How about you act like it, and give me my inheritance now so that I can get out of here and do what I want?" The father, infinitely patient and loving, forks it over, and Junior takes off. His older brother stays on, working the farm and being a good boy. When Junior has blown the loot, he finds himself impoverished and hungry, friendless and lonely. Thus begins his education. "I am a wretch," he thinks. "Although I am unworthy of membership in my father's family, I know him to be a good man. I think I'll try my luck at getting work with him." He heads for home. Meanwhile, his older brother has been faithfully drudging on his father's farm all the while.

Don't miss this. When Junior is spotted on the dusty road, Dad, overjoyed to see his prodigal returning,

---

[4]. I am deeply indebted to the late Robert Capon for his reading of this parable, not to mention a multitude of other parables found in his landmark work, *Kingdom, Grace, Judgment: Paradox, Outrage, and Vindication in the Parables of Jesus.* (See Bibliography.) His articulation of the doctrines of grace continues to ring, a clarion call to humble hearts.

doesn't really care why he is back. He doesn't wait on the deck for an explanation or an apology. He doesn't sit on the throne of judgment and moralize or teach. He runs to his son, weeping, and embraces him. "You are my son," he contends. "I thought you were lost for good, but here you are in my home again. Let's have a party and celebrate. The family is whole!"

When the older brother hears the racket, he is incensed. Why should his ne'er-do-well younger brother get a party after what he did? He did nothing to deserve it. He seethes inwardly, reasoning that his own faithful labor entitles him to the barbecue bash instead.

Can you see that both the boys had it wrong? There was not a dime's worth of difference between them. They believed that their family membership and identity was associated with their work. They saw their relationships with their dad as that of employer and employee. The younger considered himself unworthy of family membership because he had not worked; the elder thought himself worthy because he had. They both suffered from the same errant presupposition: their belonging hinged on their performance.

Their father, however, saw their family membership not in their work, but in their birth. He had fathered them; they belonged. Work had nothing to do with it. They were not employees or hirelings; they were sons, which explains why he responded as he did. He gave the prodigal his signet ring, the one stamped with the family monogram, and to the elder brother, he replied, "All that I have is yours."

"Don't you get it?" he seemed to say. "You are, both of you, my sons, because I am your father. That is what makes you family – that and not your behavior, your work ethic, or anything else." Those of us who feverishly labor to win an identity may find peace in this story. Identity is already ours. It is rooted, not in our performance, nor our many efforts to serve the miniature gods that we pursue for identity. It is rooted in the true God, the one who fathered us and who says, running to meet us, receiving us while we are still covered with the filth of our misguided pursuits to establish an identity apart from Him, "My child has returned! The family is whole! Let's have a party!" We miss the party when we approach education as an identity or a role-playing game. Education, a process which requires the painful discovery of the self, leads us to the corollary "Other," that good Father in whom we find our true selves. This discovery and its subsequent implications about identity are what really make hearts merry.

Who am I? The ragamuffin evangelist Brennan Manning says: "I am the one whom Jesus loves." This foundational identity, once discovered, becomes a definitive lens through which to view all the other relationships and roles in our lives. For we perform a multiplicity of functions. To my husband, I am wife; to my children, mother; to my parents, a daughter; to my neighbors, a friend; to my competitors, a colleague; to my students, a teacher; to my readers, an author; and so on; and so on. For any one of these roles to become my central identity, others must inevitably suffer. When any one of them becomes paramount in my understanding of self, I find that "self" in jeopardy. What happens to the teacher when she loses her job or retires? What happens to the mother when her children grow up and move away? What happens to the wife when the husband passes away unexpectedly?

Positional relationships are subject to change, and when they do, we seem to lose ourselves. Unless identity is rooted in something unchangeable, then we will forever be forced to invent and re-invent ourselves. However, when we find our identities in the unchangeable person of Christ, we perceive our other roles as functional. Rid of their misuse, they cease to be gods and become what they were designed to be – activities and blessings.

Church Father Augustine wrote, "[R]estless is our heart until it comes to rest in Thee."[5] We search for meaning, for identity, for vision, for purpose in the things of the world and the stuff of our lives when all that we seek is really found in the person of God. Once our restless hearts find their berth in the safe haven of the Father's love, everything else comes into focus.

Should education be understood as a pathway to identity, then it ought in some way to point us to this primal relationship. When it is pursued as the source of identity itself, it becomes unfruitful, unproductive, even destructive.

---

5. Aurelius Augustine, *Confessions*, ed. Albert C. Outler, Ph.D., D.D. U of Penn Linguistics Dept., 10, www.ling.upenn.edu/courses/hum100/augustinconf.pdf.

Chapter 5

Blind Guides: Identity Confusion and the Homeschool Mom

> "'Leave them; they are blind guides. If the blind lead the blind, both will fall into a pit" (Matthew 15:14).
>
> "Mr. Head could have said to it that age was a choice blessing and that only with years does a man enter into that calm understanding of life that makes him a suitable guide for the young. This, at least, had been his own experience."[1]

Let's face it. It was a set up.

I had embarked on the enterprise of home education for good reasons. Love motivated me to sacrifice for the benefit of my children. Convinced that homeschooling was the best option for them, I gave up the pursuit of a

---

1. Flannery O'Connor, "The Artificial Nigger" in *The Complete Stories*. (New York: Farrar, Straus and Giroux, 1971), 1.

career and chose homemaking. Yet in addition to noble motivations, there remained in my heart some unexamined intentions as well.

The fact of the matter was that my motives, however unconscious, were a mixed bag. A quest for identity was present beneath the surface of this altruism. Every measure I took to secure my children's success was augmented by my own desire to be successful. In fact, these two desires were so tangled up within me that I failed to discriminate between them. My heart was deceitful and wicked; how could I have known it? (Jeremiah 17:9)

Unexamined presuppositions like these are a favorite theme of the Southern Gothic author Flannery O'Connor. She loved placing characters who had the self-awareness of a turnip in scenes ripe for self-discovery. Their revelations often come through violent, educational encounters. For example, in her "A Good Man Is Hard to Find," a grandmother who thinks of herself as a good person comes face to face with her flawed humanity only when her family becomes a mark for a murderer! Less dramatic, yet perhaps more relatable, O'Connor's short story "Revelation" narrates an educational interlude in the life of a middle-class, middle-aged, white, Southern woman named Ruby Turpin.

Self-satisfied but anxious, Ruby sits in a doctor's office sizing up its occupants and flattering herself that she has "a little of everything and the God-given wit to use it right." One of the other patients in the room, the awkward and anti-social Mary Grace, becomes enraged by Ruby's self-important comments and loses her temper. She throws a book (ironically entitled *Human Development*) at Ruby, striking her (yet more ironically) in the eye. To punctuate the blow, Mary Grace follows the missile. She hurls herself across the room and attacks Ruby, strangling her and calling her a "warthog from hell." Ruby receives the "revelation" as if it came from God's own mouth. After the assault, Ruby sees the world differently: "Mrs. Turpin's vision suddenly reversed itself and she saw everything large instead of small." [2]

In the wake of the ordeal, Ruby returns home to her farm to tend her hogs. As she works, she wrestles with God and begins to see the truth in His violent message:

> ...*[L]ike a monumental statue coming to life, she bent her head slowly and gazed, as if through the very heart of mystery, down into the pig parlor at the hogs...They appeared to pant with a secret life. Until the sun slipped finally behind the tree line, Mrs. Turpin remained there with her gaze bent to them as if she were absorbing some abysmal life-giving knowledge.*[3]

The grunting hogs, unconscious of all but their needs and comforts, receiving everything from Ruby and squealing in the suffering she inflicts through her husbandry, become vehicles of the mysterious knowledge of dependency and creaturehood. Like the pigs, Mrs. Turpin protests in her pain; yet her humanity affords

---

2. Flannery O'Connor, "Revelation" in *The Complete Stories* (New York: Farrar, Straus and Giroux, 1971), 499.
3. O'Connor, "Revelation," 508.

Blind Guides

her more than animal response to stimuli. She can think about its Cause. Job-like, Mrs. Turpin's suffering affords her a profound moment of education and leads her ultimately to understanding, peace, and worship.

Even better perhaps than "Revelation" (despite its offensive title), "The Artificial Nigger" might be O'Connor's best work. In it, one Mr. Head, a grandfather who ironically considers himself a "suitable guide to the young," becomes himself the recipient of an education. A Dante-esque field trip to the city, which he has planned, ironically, to humble his grandson, occasions his own hellish realization that he is himself a blind guide: After shamefully forsaking and wholly alienating his boy in the misconceived object lesson, he and the child become lost in a bad part of town. They wander, silent and miserable, until they come upon a piece of yard art, a chipped statue of an Afro-American slave that entrances them both:

> *They stood gazing at the artificial Negro as if they were faced with some great mystery, some monument to another's victory that brought them together in their common defeat. They could both feel it dissolving their differences like an action of mercy. Mr. Head had never known before what mercy felt like because he had been too good to deserve any, but he felt he knew now.*[4]

Like Moses and the Israelites who looked upon the brass

---
4. O'Connor, "The Artificial Nigger," 269.

snake in the wilderness for healing, Mr. Head and his grandson look upon this Southern symbol of suffering, this Christ-figure, and are reconciled.

The text of this biblical story is found in Numbers 21:5-9. The wandering Israelites are visited by poisonous serpents. Bitten, many die. On behalf of the Israelites, Moses appeals to God for help. God tells him to forge an image of a brass serpent, to lift it high upon a pole, and to cause the dying people to look upon it. All who look upon it are healed; those who do not, perish.

This historical event foreshadows the crucifixion with poetic imagery, functioning as a type of Christ and the covenant that was to come through Him and His deeds. The passive gaze of the Israelites references the passive righteousness imputed to all believers who gaze upon the crucified Christ in faith for salvation. Likewise, the plaster cast of the negro slave performs a similar function for Mr. Head and his grandson. A caricature of the scapegoats upon whose striped backs the South was forged, the emblem of the slave simultaneously symbolizes the larger scapegoat Christ Jesus, who bore the sins of the world upon His own striped back, reconciling the world to God, and man to man in His sacrificial act of suffering on the cross.

The mysterious effects of this plaster figure humble Mr. Head and his grandson, and they return home wiser than they had left.

Mr. Head stood very still and felt the action of mercy touch him again but this time he knew that there were no words in the world that could name it. He understood that it grew out of agony, which is not denied to any man and which is given in strange ways to children. He understood it was all a man could carry into death to give his Maker and he suddenly burned with shame that he had so little of it to take with him. He stood appalled, judging himself with the thoroughness of God, while the action of mercy covered his pride like a flame and consumed it. He had never thought himself a great sinner before but he saw now that his true depravity had been hidden from him lest it cause him despair. He realized that he was forgiven for sins from the beginning of time, when he had conceived in his own heart the sin of Adam, until the present, when he had denied poor Nelson. He saw that no sin was too monstrous for him to claim as his own, and since God loved in proportion as He forgave, he felt ready at that instant to enter Paradise.[5]

Just like Ruby Turpin and the grandmother, Mr. Head's experience produces self-knowledge, which, upon reflection, leads to a humble wisdom and piety. The experience, even at his advanced age, is nothing less than a coming of age.

📖

Like an O'Connor short story, my experience in homeschooling was a kind of divine mercy killing. Like Mr. Head, I considered myself a qualified guide to youth, but discovered in the journey that I was only a blind guide. Like Mrs. Turpin, I worried over my place in the cosmic hierarchy and engaged in vain and presumptuous comparisons. Like the grandmother, only a violent shock would disrupt my world order enough to bring me to new self-knowledge.

Homeschooling is a noble enterprise, and I chose it for noble reasons. I suppose I thought that the combination of these truths somehow made me noble. The only trouble was that once I had embarked upon homeschooling, I was there. I found that I was the fly in the noble homeschooling ointment, the muck that fouled the virtuous water. However noble the project, my sin was bound to intrude.

When I reached the stage of our homeschooling venture when everyone was involved, all six of my children participating and me responsible for teaching every class at grade level, I began to founder. My personal expectations for performance began to press me. In the subject of literature alone one year, I taught 36 titles. Each day, I taught math for two-and-a-half hours. In addition, each of my kids was involved in an extra-curricular activity, but none of them were drivers; consequently, my husband and I had to hire an extra driver just to get them all to their various games and practices. I remember in those dark-night-of-the-soul years, when the "overwhelm" was growing to immense proportions and the sheer weight of the project was crushing me, I frequently sighed, "I want to go to Tuscany!" Peaceful landscapes and sundrenched fields called to me in my stress. Escapism seemed a great solution to the problem.

Had I managed a trip to Tuscany, however, it wouldn't have helped. The problem was that once in Tuscany, I would still have been there! Location cannot change human nature. In the same way that a trip to Tuscany would not have fixed my problems, throwing myself into the wholesome and godly world of homeschooling could not produce a wholesome or godly me. Not only that, but it could not produce wholesome and godly children. As the teenage years intruded and my children began their own searches for identity, the struggles intensified. Homeschooling did not prevent any of these conflicts. What it did do, however, was provide a landscape replete with scenarios and opportunities in which to see myself and my children as sinners who needed saving.

What did we need saving from? Mostly ourselves, as it turns out. I, for one, am most often my own worst enemy. I need saving from my presuppositions – about self, life, love, belonging, and even God. Most of the time, I get it all wrong: like Ruby Turpin and Mr. Head, I think that performance secures place. Like the older brother and the prodigal son, I confuse identity with activity and believe that belonging comes in direct proportion to productivity, usefulness, good decisions, and success.

This performance economy fills me with both fear and expectation. I fear that I am not performing well enough, even as I look for payment for the hard work I do accomplish. Like the vineyard workers in another of Jesus' notable parables, I get to the end of the workday with my hand out and my books open, ready to count the take.[6] When it does not amount to what I think I have earned, I pout, blame-shift, doubt myself, doubt God, and stew in my general resentment.

So, at the end of the homeschooling day, what did I think I had earned? Well a gold star, of course! I was looking for an A. Hard work and dedication, self-sacrifice and diligence deserve some sort of compensation, right? I was looking for the reward, the well-done good and faithful servant, the honor due the good workman.

A type-A personality, I work with drive, intensity, and focus. I attacked homeschooling just like I had attacked my own studies, with a furious fervor and persistent energy that overwhelmed everyone, myself included. Right from the start, I was all in. We lived homeschooling. Everything that we did was coordinated with learning goals. Our life was a unit study.

By the time my eldest was in the second grade, I had started teaching him Latin, which sounds unremarkable

---

6. Matthew 20:1-16. Jesus tells a parable of some laborers hired to work in a lord's vineyard. They contract for a specified wage and work all day. Meanwhile, the lord returns to the market mid-day and hires more men to add to the labor force. At the day's end, he pays all the laborers an equal wage. Of course, those who worked longest fuss about justice. Yet, the lord maintains his right to be generous with the late-comers. After all, it is his money, and he can lavish it on whom he will. Jesus utilizes the parable to infer the mercy of God on all repentant sinners. Not only those who labor long in the Lord's vineyard will receive his mercy, but all who "contract" with him receive his lavish grace. With this parable, Jesus artfully separates God's mercy from man's earnings, suggesting a better kind of economy.

until I add that I had never taken Latin myself. That was not going to stand in my way. I would learn it with him. All I needed was a book and the determination to stay a chapter or two ahead of him. When he hit third grade, I decided that he needed a peer group to chant the Latin declensions and conjugations with, so I started a co-op. Note that I did not just offer a Latin class to the neighborhood kids. Instead, I conceived of a co-operative homeschool in which each parent would participate by offering his or her gifts to the group. I saw it as perfectly in keeping with Paul's teaching about the church body and its differing gifts in 1 Corinthians. You know, each joint supplying the needs of the body. You get the idea. The co-op grew within our church until it was larger than the classical Christian day school my husband ran locally. As a result, friends and neighbors in the community began looking to us for leadership in homeschooling and educational philosophy. Of course, we gladly complied. Everything I did in regard to educating my children I did as if my life depended upon it; because in my own understanding, it did.

Meanwhile, my family was growing and with it the pressure. For a decade, I was always either pregnant or nursing – sometimes simultaneously. As my family grew, my classroom grew. The curriculum grew. The daily duties grew. My laundry grew.

Let us pause for a moment to talk about the laundry. It stood in the corner of our laundry room, a testament, a monument, to my failure. No matter how diligently I attacked the pile, it never grew any smaller. Artist Todd

Wilson's apt cartoon depicts this phenomenon. It pictures a mother, bleary eyed, holding a basket of neatly folded clothes, while her son bounds into the next frame with arms full of laundry saying something like, "Coming through! Can't remember if these are clean or dirty!" I used to joke that I was sure I would die in a pile of dirty laundry. Once, I threw my back out reaching for a sock to fold. As I lay, paralyzed by painful spasms, I thought, here it is – a self-fulfilling prophecy.

The laundry is a neat metaphor for law in this scenario. The law of keeping up with the laundry, having a shiny, clean laundry room that smells nice and drawers full of neatly folded clothes in every room, judged me and found me lacking. In my mind, laundry was shorthand for homemaking. If the laundry was done, I was succeeding as a homemaker. If it was not, I was failing. The problem was, my success or failure varied on a moment by moment basis. No matter how hard I worked to keep the "law of laundry," success evaded me, receding into the future indefinitely. It was hopeless.

What does laundry have to do with homeschooling? Well, it is obvious, isn't it? Homeschooling. Home-schooling. It happens at home as an extension of my work as a homemaker and mother. The responsibilities of homemaking did not stop because I was educating my kids. They were merely complicated by it. Not only that, but according to the unit study mentality by which all of my activities were organically unified with my homeschooling efforts, I imported the added condemnation that the problem existed because I was failing to train my children in the art of home management. According to the experts, they ought to have been becoming a little army of diligent house-workers who facilitated the Martha Stewart ideal I held in my mind's eye. They were, however, just kids. What they did really well was make messes and laundry – piles of laundry. What they did really well was demonstrate to this type A mom how underequipped she was to keep up with the standard. What they were, in this and every other application, was a blessing. They were God's severe mercy to me. They were killing me, leaving my visions of perfection strewn in ruins everywhere, and the laundry was just an index of the event.

📖

During the early years of homeschooling when I was juggling babies and school-aged children, I kept my schoolroom on the landing of our three-story home. While I was teaching the older kids upstairs, I would hear the younger ones, running around screaming, raising themselves like wolves in the basement playroom. The competing expectations of motherhood for the two different age groups presented a conundrum. In order to be a good preschool mommy, I ought to have been downstairs supervising, creating play opportunities, and practicing "mindfulness" so that I would not "miss it." On the other hand, in order to be a good elementary homeschool parent, I needed to be creating an atmosphere conducive to learning, to be drilling my youngsters in their times tables, reading aloud to them, teaching them their phonogram flashcards and spelling, and helping them to develop lovely handwriting. Anyone who has tried to do this knows firsthand that these two paradigms are hard to fit together. Just by virtue of the impossibility of being in two places at the same time, I was foiled before I began. There was no way to be perfect here.

At other, older homeschool veterans' suggestions, I created things like homeschool toy boxes to be opened only while I was teaching. The idea was that these toys would hold a fascination for the little ones that would keep them rapt with enjoyment and quietly playing in the corner while I gave my undivided attention to teaching the older kids. Sounds like a good idea, right? It didn't work for me either. Instead, I taught math facts while changing diapers. I explained the proper rules that governed the use of a silent final 'e' while separating two spatting pre-schoolers. I fought to focus through a reading lesson while a lively game of "Missy and Adam" (my kids' version of "house") unfolded in the corner.

When there really was a moment of silence, I would look up from whatever I was finally getting done with inner dread. Where had they gone? What were they into now? At such times I discovered my toddler covered in my brand new lipstick, with which he was coloring, crayon-like, on the carpet. Or I found him sitting in a pile of powdered laundry soap, with which he had invented his own sandbox. Or I discovered him fast asleep on the threshold of the back door, having cried himself to sleep when his siblings had bounded in, slamming the door behind them. He was too short to work the handle. Poor lamb.

I could go on, but in truth, these moments – we can laugh now, because we're all okay – hurt my heart. They were parenting debacles on my part, moments when I failed to be mindful, present, available, aware, omniscient, and omnipresent.

"But wait," you say, "those qualities belong to God alone!" Exactly. In the words of my one-time college advisor, I was getting what you might call an education. I was figuring out what manner of creature I was, and I fell short of even my own expectations. I was a limited creature, not a god, and the evidence was everywhere. I did not have it all together.

■

As the kids grew older, our homeschooling settled into a gentle rhythm. Since I thrive on structure, our school grew orderly. I thrive on books, so our efforts bore the stamp of scholarship. The kids were learning to read, to figure, to experiment, to explore; they were learning to learn.

They were, however, also learning to interpret their experiences in the same way I interpreted mine: as evidence of their value, mementos of their identity. For one child, this meant that every time she failed at math, she personally was a failure. For another, it meant adopting a know-it-all stance, because knowing meant belonging, being Somebody. (This is a real obstacle to learning, by the way, having to pretend that you already know. The precondition for learning, after all, is the ability to admit ignorance.) For another, it meant lying and cheating on assignments for fear that his own work would not be good enough. For another, it meant trying, and trying harder to secure standing, even while knowing that the next assignment could negate all the identity his hard work had earned. What I created was a house full of performers and legalists, and I did it just by effective modeling.

Meanwhile, the kids looked pretty good to outsiders. I mean, they are great kids, wonderful people. They were respectful, obedient, and they cleaned up pretty well. They looked adults in the eye and called them by their surname. They did their homework, mastered material, and made the grades. Our school whirred along, buzzing with activity, bearing all the signs of real education — and I do not mean to denigrate the learning that was occurring despite us. They learned. They grew. They became upstanding citizens in the area. They aced their SATs and earned scholarships to college. They were successes.

When my eldest received his college acceptance letter with a hefty scholarship, my heart swelled with pride. He had done it! We had done it! I had done it! It was an uphill battle, but we made it. Victory was ours. Not only that, but he would go to my own alma mater, sit in the same classrooms that his father and I had frequented and under many of the same profs. In the secret of my heart

I could see the scenario: He raises his hand. He gives a profound answer to some difficult question, and the prof responds, "Who taught you that?" To which my son, guileless, would respond, "Oh, I was homeschooled." I would get my gold star. He would gain a reputation for intelligence. Everyone would be happy.

Except that's just not how it went down.

Chapter 6

The Death of Kings:
Relationships and Homeschooling

> *"And when He came near the gate of the city, behold, a dead man was being carried out, the only son of his mother...When the Lord saw her, He had compassion on her and said to her, 'Do not weep.' Then He came and touched the open coffin, and those who carried him stood still. And He said, 'Young man, I say to you, arise.' And he who was dead sat up and began to speak. And He presented him to his mother"* (Luke 7:12-15).
>
> *"For God's sake let us sit upon the ground and tell sad stories of the death of kings..."* (Richard II, 3.2.155-156).

Recently, I had opportunity to ask my grown children their most and least favorite things about homeschooling. After thinking a moment, my middle son Aaron responded, "The best thing about homeschooling is that your mom is your teacher; the worst is that your mom is your teacher." I thought that statement was pretty profound, a good summary of the issue.

It is very hard to wear both hats, both for the children and for the mom. As a mother, you are called to love unconditionally, never allowing your evaluation of your child's performance to color their understanding of your love for them. Selfless service is what is needed here, which is actually rather seductive.

Not long ago, I saw a sign posted to advertise a school levy in our area, which occasioned a revealing inner dialogue. It read: "Our kids are worth whatever it takes." The sign authors were speaking, of course, about money. Few of them, I reasoned, would concede to quitting their nine-to-fives and schooling their kids themselves; so, not whatever it takes. Really, they meant the kids are worth whatever money it takes, and all the better if it is someone else's money. Reasoning thus inwardly, I felt rather smug and figured that I had made the real sacrifice, giving up the chance at a second income and shouldering the daily burden in order to give my kids a private education.

On the other hand, what giving the kids this kind of education demanded of both them and me was constant evaluation. It was my job to mark up their essays in red pencil, to raise the bar, to demand excellence. I was the one with my foot in their backs telling them that only their very best would be good enough to earn them a scholarship or win them their dream job.

The cognitive dissonance created by this multi-tasking poses one of the greatest challenges of homeschooling: How shall we maintain the sanctity of the home as a place of affirmation, acceptance, and approval while simultaneously maintaining a high bar of academic standards? How shall we create a culture of grace in a culture of performance?

I reconciled this dissonance with the Bible verse, "and whatever you do, do it heartily, as to the Lord, and not to men..." (Colossians 3:23). Unfortunately, I myself was deaf to the second part of that verse, "as to the Lord, and not to men." In my own attempts to define myself through my activities, to create identity for myself through personal achievements, I had become, however unwittingly, a man-pleaser. Consequently, in my fast pursuit of the praises of men, I was raising a house full of man-pleasers, and this was not their fault. It was mine. The fear of man had indeed become, as the proverbist uttered, a snare. (Proverbs 29:25) It complicated everything.

This conundrum reached its apex when my eldest son approached high school graduation and faced the college application process. It was a time fraught with fear and anxiety for me, which perversion you might notice immediately. It seemed imperative that he perform well on standardized tests since we had homeschooled independently throughout his primary and secondary education. There needed to be some validation of his homeschool GPA that was universally acceptable so that the institutions to which he applied knew the meaning of our grading scale. His father and I made him take the SAT three times, even though he performed well on the first, each time hoping to improve his position.

In addition, we were attached to the idea of him

attending a particular college because of its commitment to the liberal arts, to the Western heritage, and to the Permanent Things. We were convinced that it was the best choice in higher education. This, too, was complicated because it was also our alma mater. From our son's perspective, we were pushing him to go to our school, rather than allowing him to just be himself. We assured him that, once on campus, if he was not happy, we would gladly help him transfer. Finally, because we were a single income family with six kids, it would be necessary for him to win a scholarship to defray the expense of the thing.

What a lot of pressure was placed on this kid! If you add to these things the unspoken perception that his performance in these matters had the potential to prove not only his own, but also his mother's life's work a success or a failure, the situation was volatile in the extreme.

When the acceptance letter and scholarship offer came, I had, in the back of my mind, in seedling form in my heart, the notion that the other shoe was set to drop. It appeared that we had achieved the dream, but I was dealing with recurrent nightmares. God was speaking to me in my sleep, and in quiet tones He was reassuring me that I had not gone unnoticed. I was not alone. I was not my own god. He was, as always, the great I AM, and I was the apple of His eye. What is more, He never sleeps, but works constantly on my behalf, bringing me to self-knowledge and driving me to the seat of His mercy, the foot of the cross of the crucified Jesus. This situation would prove no exception.

A few weeks before my son left for college, the pressure became too great for him. He dropped on us what felt at the time like a bomb. In a private and totally unanticipated conversation with his father, he announced that he thought he hated him. My mild-mannered and loving husband, the man who had given himself to fathering with the same intensity with which I had attacked my work in the home, was devastated and confused. How had this happened? From the moment our son's life began, we had organized our priorities around him. We had loved him and worked to provide him with every good thing. How had our sweet and smiling, open-hearted boy become so bitter, rebellious, and angry? When had he decided that we were the enemy? Why was he choosing this auspicious moment to act out of his anger, and what would he do in his state? In retrospect, the fact that this came as any sort of a surprise is astonishing. We had provoked our son, however unintentionally, to wrath. Of course he was angry.

We debated at the time about whether to put the brakes on sending him off to school. It was states away, and we feared that in his frame of mind, he might do something foolish. Nevertheless, my husband felt strongly that it was time for the boy to go and have an experience in the world outside our home. However painful the experience might be, it was bound to produce good fruit in the long run. We must trust the Lord. The whole family trekked cross-country by car to drop him off at school. He was foul in temper, communicating to us all that he would just as soon we leave and let him get on with the business of living his own life.

That first semester was brutal. He and I had always been close. We are both verbal communicators, and had spent hours talking together about anything and everything during his childhood. Although we share intense personalities, we had sparred good naturedly over the years, our adversarial relationship the subject of many a family joke. He knew all of my buttons and delighted in playing what he termed "whack-a-mole in the button room" with me. Now, suddenly, the communication ceased. I received only one call from him that first semester, and I never allowed myself to call him. I felt his unspoken need for silence and space and somehow managed to honor it.

When we visited him for Parent's Weekend that first semester, he knew every student on campus. Socially, at least, he was thriving. What we heard from the faculty, however, (in not so many words) was a bit less encouraging. They were worried about him, about his health. They were not sure he was sleeping much. He might be having difficulty adjusting to the scheduling demands of an academic lifestyle. He fell asleep in class and scored low on quizzes. This is, of course, all euphemistic code language for rebellion and intemperance.

By the time his first semester was over, his GPA reflected these things despite the fact that he was receiving the second largest merit award on campus. When we addressed the issue during his Christmas vacation, he assured us that he could and would do better. While we knew that he could, we were less certain that he would, and he validated our skepticism with an even lower GPA second semester. By some act of mercy, the college did not take away his academic scholarship. No doubt, they had seen this before. They believed in him.

The immovable law was coming to bear on our son, but the law cannot produce that which it demands. It would seek him out and expose him so that he could see himself at last, and he was not the only one who experienced vulnerability in this process. He was not the only one who felt the probing accusation of the law. I, too, was exposed. This was a far cry from the scenario I had imagined in my secret self. You remember it, the scene in which his teachers would remark on his brilliance and award me with a gold star for the superior education and preparation he had received at home.

By the time Ian made it home for summer break, I was contemplating throwing in the proverbial homeschooling towel. His siblings would certainly be better off in a day school, I murmured. Even a public school would be better than what I had managed to achieve. These words, however, belied my presuppositions, which had not changed a bit. Performancism remained at the root of my perception.

All that had changed was that I suddenly saw myself not as a Can, but a Can't, and this new identity was weighted with all the accompanying self-pity you might expect. Not only that, but it communicated to my son with new force that he was still what he did. He was failing his classes; he was a failure. With tears in his eyes, my son begged me not to add to the guilt of his own bad behavior the responsibility of derailing his siblings' education. Homeschooling was not the problem, he said. He was the problem. He had misconstrued everything. He had attributed to us things we did not mean. He had accused us of trying to control his life when we only intended to help him grow and learn. He had rebelled against a law that we had not erected.

I wish it were so. He thought too well of me. "Do not provoke your children to wrath," the scriptures admonish, but wrath is what I had driven him to, my noble intentions notwithstanding. It was all my fault. I had raised him to fear man. I had raised him to confuse work and identity. I had pushed him to the breaking point. Although he hesitated to attribute this sin to me at the time, it was mine. Despite all of my best efforts, I had set us both up for a fall.

My work with my children was my gift to them, but like all the gifts of man, it was fraught with sin. Like the coiled, clay serpent I'd shaped on his first day of school, the one that scared him to death and left us both crying, the snake in my gift had struck us both, and we were dying. We stood like the Israelites, gazing upon the bronze serpent for healing. We stood like Mr. Head and his grandson, gazing at the scapegoat, transfixed by the suffering, waiting on the mysterious miracle to do its work.

The scriptures say that God lays low so that He can restore. He destroys so that He can rebuild, and the destruction of my paradigm, this blow to my presuppositions regarding the source of identity, was really the beginning of a new vision of self and others. This vision, rooted in the gospel of grace, would liberate me from the exhausting pursuit of identity and find me safely home, just one of the family, loved by the God who bore me and my sins.

My son's story smacks of this grace, too, but it is his story, and I prefer to let him tell it. Maybe we will share together someday – two perspectives on the same experience. Come to think of it, maybe not. It would probably just provoke from the audience the timeless question: How can we avoid this ourselves? A fruitless question to which I respond, "Why would you want to do that?!" Because listen to what happened next:

My son, my husband, and I were each forced to look at ourselves. We could not help but find that our own hands had worked this disaster. For my part, I could see that my quest for identity had polluted my homeschooling efforts. The fact that I had homeschooled for the kids' benefit was not the only operative truth. There was "self" present in my actions as well. The self never really dies. It is like the villain in the horror flick that appears to be dead on the floor, but that lunges up out of nowhere with a knife for a final go at you.

I love my kids, and because they are among the few things in the world that I really do love more than myself, this experience was what it took to lay me bare. Despite all my labor, careful planning, self-denial, and faithful diligence, I had fouled up everything. My own quest for identity had damaged their understanding of their own. I had become not the hero, but the villain in my children's story.

Sadly, my children were not the only victims on the scene. There was collateral damage in our homeschooling co-op as well. For there, I had nurtured a climate of performancism by erecting a metaphorical temple to the god of academics. Brennan Manning suggests that in your quest for identity, whatever you serve that is smaller than God is an idol.[1] We served academics. In the co-op we had established, Adam and I reflected, we had served as high priest and priestess, making sacrifices day and night to a false god. Everyone involved was affected by the stench of our idolatry. No relationship was immune from the toxic atmosphere that accompanied this relentless pursuit of identity.

Can you see the economy of death at work in my flesh? (I told you this was going to be the story of a divine mercy killing.) Yet even as the Lord allowed the consequences of my sin to kill me, He was at work in another economy, resurrecting me and my family to newness of life. True to His nature, He is in the business of making beauty out of ashes, making dead men live, and making the wrath of man to praise Him.

The new economy I reference is that of grace, and it looks like this: He takes my failure, the trail of ruin and devastation wrought by my best efforts, and He exchanges it for His perfection. He receives my poor performance, my sin-ridden self, with a "well done, good

---

1. In his *Posers, Fakers, and Wannabes: Unmasking the Real You*, Mannan states, "The tiny gods we worship when we draw back from the true God are idols we've made to look just like us" (21).

and faithful servant," which is really, as the rest of that verse indicates, an invitation to "enter into the rest of the Lord." I get paid, not according to the books I have so carefully kept, but according to the foreign economy of grace. Out of the abundance of His mercy and righteousness, God gives, loves boundlessly, and rewards His unprofitable servants with the riches His own hands have wrought. Meanwhile, if we question the legitimacy of His bookkeeping or cry for an audit, He smiles and reminds us that He can do what He wants. After all, it is His money. If He is interested in wasting Himself on poor souls like us, then who is to argue with Him?

The homeschool is a perfect lab in which to observe the action of grace. It is one of God's greatest classrooms. There, everybody learns. Even parents get a "second chance" at their own education. I said this for years before I really came to know what it meant. By education, I guess I had in mind pretentious self-improvement, rather than a disabusing encounter with my censurable self. I had no idea what that education was going to mean, because I had yet to discover what true education was.

Home is the perfect environment in which to come to know and be known. There, as your experiences and your studies reveal to you the manner of creature you are – the finitude and the poverty, the grandeur and the misery of your own condition – you gain empathy for those who, like you, carry the common curse. You discover the love of the God who made you and learn that you belong, not because of your striving, but because of your Father. In fellowship together with your children, mired with sins you cannot disguise, you learn to repent and to forgive and discover that, in spite of yourself, you are both fully known and fully loved. In this process, you discover the truth of Lewis's unsavory assertion in *The Great Divorce*: "Shame is like that. If you will accept it – if you will drink the cup to the bottom – you will find it very nourishing: but try to do anything else with it and it scalds." [2]

I'd love to say that my response to my son's rebellion was immediate confession and repentance; however, that credit goes to his father. Far from angry, Adam's response to Ian's hatred was repentance and sorrow. He listened and asked for understanding. He confessed that, although he didn't understand, he wanted to. He told Ian that he knew himself fully capable of the kind of behavior that would inspire rebellion, and that he was so sorry for whatever he had done.

I came along behind my husband slowly. My years of effort and "good behavior" formed an opaque obstacle between me and self-sight. God was dealing with me as Emily Dickinson relates in her poem 46: "He fumbles at your spirit as players at the keys before they drop full music on; He stuns you by degrees..." My understanding of my role in our family drama developed gradually. It would be years before I saw myself in this matter, and when I did, years more before I realized the need to narrate my discoveries to my son. Unless I'm mistaken,

---

2. C.S. Lewis, *The Great Divorce* (San Francisco: HarperCollins, 2001), 61.

this final step has restored our relationship and liberated him from the bondage of shame that enveloped him as well, setting him free from the performance identity he'd earned through his own failure. Love is liberating.

The discovery of mutual need, common sin, and failure levels the playing field between parents and children and becomes a source of genuine fellowship, deep relationship. Like the mother in the scriptures who followed the coffin of her dead son, I was pitied by my Lord, and He restored my son to life and to me. In the process of death and resurrection, my son had become a man. He is a wonderful man. I do not deserve him. God's mercy is overwhelming.

Chapter 7

Mad Men and Pasteboard Masks: Rebellious Creatures and the Hidden God

> *"Hark ye yet again,–the little lower layer. All visible objects, man, are but as pasteboard masks. But in each event—in the living act, the undoubted deed—there, some unknown but still reasoning thing puts forth the mouldings of its features from behind the unreasoning mask."*[1]

Some of you may be reacting to my narrative with something like this: *That's it? After all the dramatic build-up, the big devastating deal is that the kid rebelled?* The very fact that I considered this a wonder is telling. Why are parents of homeschoolers so surprised when their teens rebel? Teenage rebellion is so ubiquitous as to have

---

1. Herman Melville, *Moby Dick; or, The Whale* in *The Great Books of the Western World* Vol. 48, ed. Mortimer J. Adler et al. (Chicago: Encyclopaedia Britannica, 1990), 75.

become a kind of trope; yet we are shocked to discover it within the borders of our own communities and families. We think that because we have taught our kids the Law of God, kept them from the world and laid our lives down for them, they (and by extension – we) will be immune from the rebellion that's common to the teen years. Some are. I'd hazard a guess that the ratio of those who rebel to those who do not is about the same proportionately inside the church as out. Christianity certainly doesn't prevent men from sinning.

Why do so many Christian teens rebel? Why do so many teens rebel? We might as well ask why so many people rebel. We rebel because we are human. Rebellion is one of the two primal reactions to the Law, which was designed to expose man's sinful nature – and it's really good at it.

In the Apostle Paul's second letter to the Corinthians, he writes that "the letter kills, but the Spirit gives life" (2 Corinthians 3:6). Furthermore, he calls the Law the "ministry of death" (v.7) and the "ministry of condemnation," (v. 9) never gainsaying its glory, but only elucidating its purpose. The Law cannot save man, but only condemns him. In response to the Law, men either rebel or perform. In light of the message of the gospel, even performance is rebellion in disguise – a refusal to bank on the righteousness of Christ and a determination to earn God's acceptance by our independent actions.

Educators often remark on the humanizing effect of the liberal arts. Certainly, the literary classics provide countless examples of man's penchant for rebelling

Mad Men and Pasteboard Masks

against the limits of his own humanity. Man likes agency, and when faced with the reality of his subjectivity and creaturehood, rebellion is a knee-jerk response. Consider Captain Ahab in Melville's *Moby Dick*, who discovered his humanity in his encounter with the infamous white whale, losing a limb in the process. His response? Rage. Rage and a vindictive determination to confront the beast and pull back the "pasteboard mask" that concealed the Motive Force beneath. Starbuck, his pious first-mate, calls him mad: "'Vengeance on a dumb brute!' cried Starbuck, 'that simply smote thee from blindest instinct! Madness! To be enraged with a dumb thing, Captain Ahab, seems blasphemous.'" [2] Yet, make no mistake. Ahab wasn't crazy; he was only mad – furious to discover that he wasn't in control after all. He says as much in his response to Starbuck:

Hark ye yet again, —the little lower layer. All visible objects, man, are but as pasteboard masks. But in each event—in the living act, the undoubted deed—there, some unknown but still reasoning thing puts forth the mouldings of its features from behind the unreasoning mask. If man will strike, strike through the mask! How can the prisoner reach outside except by thrusting through the wall? To me, the white whale is that wall, shoved near to me. Sometimes I think there's naught beyond. But 'tis enough. He tasks me; he heaps me; I see in him outrageous strength, with an inscrutable malice sinewing it. That

---

2. Melville, *Moby Dick*, 74.

inscrutable thing is chiefly what I hate; and be the white whale agent, or be the white whale principal, I will wreak that hate upon him.[3]

Unlike Starbuck, who took his creaturehood seriously and submitted to the "inscrutable thing" with religious genuflection, Ahab set himself against it and went down with the ship. We can see in these two characters the types of the rebel and the performer, and notice that, actually, neither gets it right. Both ultimately meet their deaths. While Ahab rages, pursuing God, Starbuck superstitiously avoids Him, carefully keeping himself to avoid death by detection.

When confronted by our own white whales, do we rage like Ahab? Do our children? Or do we respond religiously, hoping our good behavior and pious devotion will engender God's good favor, turn away His wrath? Until we know the heart of the God who hunts us, rebellion or performancism will be our response to Him. Both assert our agency. Both leave us insecure, fearful, and angry. Both, ultimately, lead us to death.

The story of Ahab demonstrates that becoming acquainted with our creaturehood can be cataclysmic. When children finally experience the truth behind the witness of the humanities – when they finally discover that they themselves are human and not gods, their reactions can be violent. Homeschooling doesn't make children immune from this response to the human

---
3. Ibid., 75.

condition. In fact, attentive schooling in the liberal arts, uniquely adept at depicting and evoking the real grandeur and misery of man, may speed such a confrontation. That is to say, liberal arts homeschooling may accelerate the process of education, liberating children from the grip of childish narcissism by demonstrating to them that they are not gods, but instead gifted creatures. If they react to this discovery like Ahab, we ought not to be surprised. Rebellion is a stop on the way to self-knowledge. As such, it is not a mark of failure, but rather of progress, if it is not the final destination. Perhaps parents' dismay and confusion in the event of such rebellion result from forgetting the end goal of education – not godhood, but creaturehood – not mastery, but self-knowledge. While education cannot save an individual, it can and should demonstrate the human need for a savior.

This is why we educate: not to make our children masters of a world they can never truly control, but to make them aware of the true nature of things. We educate so that they will know who they are and who they are not – to help them discover and develop their own native gifts. (Gifts, by the way, are another indicator of creaturehood and subjectivity since they imply a Giver, who cached such within them to be discovered and developed for their good and the good of the larger community.) Christian education does not remove the humanity from kids. It does not make them superhuman. It does not eliminate their fallen nature. Instead, it targets and exposes their humanity so that they can arrive at self-knowledge in a safe environment, awakening to discover that, though fallen in nature and subject to forces larger than themselves, they are both known and loved. This is the desperate longing of the human heart – to know the face behind the pasteboard mask, and be we Ahabs or Starbucks, our lives will be shaped by what we discover there.

Chapter 8

Better Conduct: The Performer

> "When it came to such a pitch as this, she was not able to refrain from a start, or a heavy sigh, or even from walking about the room for a few seconds – and the only source whence anything like consolation or composure could be drawn, was in the resolution of her own better conduct, and the hope that, however inferior in spirit and gaiety might be the following and every future winter of her life to the past, it would yet find her more rational, more acquainted with herself, and leave her less to regret when it were gone." [1]

Man is born with performance worked into his flesh. While some rebel against the Law, others try to keep it. Now if keeping the Law were the point of Christianity, then the performers would have it made; however,

---

1. Jane Austen, *Emma* in *The Great Books of the Western World Vol. 46*, ed. Mortimer J. Adler et al. (Chicago: Encyclopaedia Britannica, 1990), 172.

Christianity is not about man's success, but his failure. It is, in fact, about man's incapability and the capability of Christ Jesus that meets it. Christianity is not about what man produces; rather, it is about what he receives as the object of God's affection.

    We get this wrong all the time. Not only do we get it wrong when we are talking about the holy and perfect Law of God, but we get it wrong when we are talking about all the "little-l" laws we erect for ourselves to prove our goodness. These might look like Emily Post's rules for etiquette or sound like the voice of your mother in your head, telling you not to leave your dirty socks on the floor or let the sun set on your dinner dishes. Regardless of the content of these laws, they have a similar effect to that of the divine Law in that they demonstrate to us our inability to perform well. Regardless of how hard we try to keep these laws, they judge us and find us lacking. Even when we think we have kept them to a degree, there is always a way to have done what they require better.

    When I was a child, my mother taught me to write a thank you note whenever someone did something nice for me. I had that in my arsenal of good behavior and had been keeping it for ages. Then I met a woman who one-upped it. I took her some cookies on a plate, and she returned my plate with a thank you note and another confection she had baked. Her mother had taught her a deeper law of reciprocity. I felt ashamed that, for years, all I had done is said thank you. Talking to her, I discovered that the law she had learned made every gift she received, every act of kindness shown to her, a burden and an expectation. Once I was aware of her expectations, I felt them myself.

That is the nature of law. It exists to demonstrate to us that we are too small to meet its demands. God's Law is designed to demonstrate our creaturehood, our finitude, our sin, and our need for Christ. The "little-l" laws we erect for ourselves tend to function in the same way. The Bible suggests that the purpose of the Law is to affect a mercy killing, and it is so well designed that we cannot escape its action. Try as we may to obey it, it will always perform its divine purpose in our lives. There is no way to evade the truth the Law is designed to reveal: God is God, and we are not.

There are two basic responses to the Law. One is to rebel against it; the other is to work hard to keep it. Really though, these two responses are synonymous. The rebel looks at the Law's demands and says, "Forget it. I'm not even going to try, and what's more, you can't make me." The performer says, "I can do that." Both responses, however, miss the point of the Law, which is not good behavior, but self-revelation.

My father-in-law, a preacher, says that the Law is not a scrub brush, but a mirror. It is designed not to clean us up, but to reflect the contents of our hearts. It exists to show us what manner of creatures we are. The Law is a testimony to the character and nature of God. As such, it exists as a signpost, directing us to the Messiah – that God-man Jesus who, by perfectly keeping the Law, demonstrated His divinity and redeemed mankind.

Whereas my son responded to the "little-l" laws of our family with rebellion, some kids respond with performance. They try to keep the law. Pleasers, they strive to earn their parents' and the world's approval through their good behavior. For the parent, this kind of a child is a real blessing. They do what they are told and do not cause trouble. They make you look good! For the child, however, this response is a mixed bag. On the one hand, they do not have to experience many negative external consequences for their behavior. They avoid disciplinary action, they earn the praises of their parents and men, and in the case of the "little-l" laws of homeschooling, they even experience some of the benefits of learning. They often excel in their studies. A majority of these kids thrive on praise, and so the more affirmation they receive, the harder they work. Praise is their drug of choice, and they strive for it.

Yet while these kids may look better on the outside than their rebel counterparts, they too experience the pain of the law's judgment; for, what is good enough? What is accomplished enough? What is smart enough? There is always another assignment, a smarter person, another subject waiting to judge them deficient in their quest for excellence. If their acceptance accrues from their performance, then they are always only one misstep away from failure and rejection. The performer is on a treadmill that just keeps going faster, and they will eventually fall off, either from fatigue or exasperation.

There does exist a third possibility: that the performer never does meet anyone smarter, faster, or better than himself, but consider: that is not necessarily a better outcome. Such is the case of *Emma*, the protagonist in Jane Austen's eponymous novel. Superior in birth, rank, and talent, she lives above her society, condescending to everyone she knows and feeling gracious for it. Austen describes her:

> *Emma is spoiled by being the cleverest of her family. At ten years old, she had the misfortune of being able to answer questions which puzzled her sister at seventeen. She was always quick and assured; Isabella slow and diffident. And ever since she was twelve, Emma has been mistress of the house and of you all. In her mother she lost the only person able to cope with her. She inherits her mother's talents, and must have been under subjection to her.*[2]

Unfortunately, Emma's mother has died, and Emma is subject to no one. For the accomplished individual, pride inevitably seeps in around the edges, and it judges them losers in the law-keeping game just like their rebel brothers. When Emma begins to see her disadvantage, she takes comfort, however cold, in the knowledge that acquaintance with herself might in the future subdue her pride, improving her character:

> *When it came to such a pitch as this, she was not able to refrain from a start, or a heavy sigh, or even from*

---

2. Austen, *Emma*, 16.

> *walking about the room for a few seconds – and the only source whence anything like consolation or composure could be drawn, was in the resolution of her own better conduct, and the hope that, however inferior in spirit and gaiety might be the following and every future winter of her life to the past, it would yet find her more rational, more acquainted with herself, and leave her less to regret when it were gone.*[3]

Yet, the marginalization of regret cannot be equated with contentment or, moreover, joy. Emma's performance does not give her peace.

Fatigue and stamina are not the performer's only problems. Consider the underlying assumption that drives them: they believe that their positional acceptance – by God, parents, friends, the world – is contingent upon their behavior. Regardless of their ability to maintain their performance, their false assumptions about belonging so cloud the issue that they become impervious to the reality of the love others do have for them. Love and relationship become, not miraculous blessings in their lives, but wages earned.

Again, Austen's *Emma* epitomizes this condition. When she realizes that her love for the superior Mr. Knightley is returned, her heart leaps in joyful gratitude. He more than any other character in the story has seen her most clearly. That he should love her still, she considers a wonder: "Within half an hour, he had passed

---

3. Austen, *Emma*, 172.

from a thoroughly distressed state of mind, to something so like perfect happiness, that it could bear no other name. Her change was equal. – This single half hour had given to each the same precious certainty of being beloved, had cleared from each the same degree of ignorance, jealousy, or distrust..." [4] To be known and loved is to find peace and joy, the closest thing to happiness in this world.

I speak from experience. If you have not yet guessed, I might as well announce that I am myself a performer. It was not until I was loved by someone with whom I had behaved in an absolutely hateful way that I ever really perceived a love that was extended to me no strings attached. It went something like this:

I have this friend who is what we Christians call a ten-talent woman. She is articulate, beautiful, smart, and funny. She has a fabulous sense of fashion and is always the life of the party. She is a successful professional and has a plethora of interesting experiences to share. For years, whenever we spent time together in a group, I left feeling like an uninteresting drudge of a washerwoman – just a stay-at-home mom. A variety of extenuating circumstances, which had nothing to do with her, worked to intensify my feelings until they were a boiling stew of angst. When the lid flew off, I found myself standing on a chair in a restaurant (metaphorically speaking) announcing to her that I hated her and never wanted to see her again.

---

4. Ibid., 176.

Where did this violent outburst originate? It came from a deep well of insecurity inside of me. Because she did not see these insecurities, she inadvertently exposed them just by being her fabulous self. I wanted her to respect me. Although I later discovered that she did (hard to imagine why after that scene), I did not seem to get the response I was looking for from her. When she did not prop up the identity I was so carefully crafting for myself, I resented her.

Gladly, the story does not end there. I told you my friend is fabulous, and she is. Listen: Not long after my dramatic proclamation, I found myself at a women's retreat, speaking about the importance of self-awareness. (I know; the irony is rich.) I was in the process of learning that transparency is the foundation of real relationship, and I was stepping out in faith to reveal the parts of me I had hidden from view all my life. After delivering what I had prepared, which included some honest confessions about my own identity building, I asked for questions from the attendees. What I got instead was a barrage of "affirmation." The ladies in the audience took the opportunity to gun me down by bearing witness to the sinful behaviors and character flaws I had confessed. "You really are like that. I have always seen that about you." Even a visitor from outside our group, a stranger to me, weighed in, saying that she had already seen those terrible things about me in the one, shallow conversation we had had that weekend. It was as if I had drawn a large target on my breast, and it was open season.

Better Conduct

When the retreat was over, I returned home and crawled under my covers, determined never to come out again. I felt like the fairytale emperor who ventured into public unclothed. All the time I had spent with these women thinking I was acceptable, I had really been walking around naked. They saw me more clearly than I saw myself.

I was devastated, sure that I was no longer acceptable to anyone. In my distress, I had the audacity to call my friend. Whatever possessed me to pick up that phone, I will never know. Of all the people in my life, she had the most cause to hammer the nails into my coffin at that moment, but she did not. Instead, she listened. She cried with me. She told me that she would love me – that she had my back. Then, she hopped in her car and drove seven hours to arrive on my doorstep with a bottle of wine and a bag of chocolates just to make sure I had heard her. That undeserved love, that act of grace, might have been the first I was ever vulnerable enough to perceive.

How is it possible that I had never received love of this sort before? I have a mother who loves me, a husband who loves me, children who love me. What gives? Well, in each of those relationships, I worked hard to make myself lovely. Although I knew I failed to love any of my people perfectly, I was always careful to make a place for myself with them. I kept a ledger of relational credits and deficits and always knew where I stood. I performed in these relationships to convince everyone, including myself, that I was a good daughter, a good wife, a good mother. This relationship with my friend was the first time in which there was no way to narrate the story that would allow me to perceive myself as good. I was not a good friend to her. I was hateful, and she had returned my hatred with love. The discontinuity of this exchange rose above the din of my fearful heart, and I heard her. Grace alone penetrated the tough shell of my performance economy.

When our performance becomes our identity, we can sometimes convince ourselves that we have earned the love we receive from others. As a result, we dismiss it. It beads up and rolls off our backs like water off a duck. We intuitively suspect that if everyone knew what we were really like, they would change their tunes, and we would find ourselves in the outer darkness. Because we suspect that the person they love is only an image we have cultivated, a fraudulent imposter,[5] we discount the love they offer.

So, in spite of appearances, performers are not in a much better position than the rebels where the security of being fully known and loved is concerned. In some ways, they are further from it than their counterparts. In the score-keeping game of performance, there are only losers; no one really wins. That is the severe mercy of God at work for us. If we could achieve identity and righteousness without God, we would all do it, but He loves us too much to allow us to miss our created pur-

---

[5]. I am indebted to Christian writer and speaker Brennan Manning for his teaching on the Imposter, presented in his classic book, *Abba's Child*. I highly recommend this book for anyone looking to understand identity.

pose in this world: to know Him and His great love for us and to enjoy Him forever.

So how does the Law affect performer-students as it works itself out in an impossibly law-driven homeschool economy? They perform their little heads off. They work, and work, and work, and work. They worry they are not good enough when they make a 98% on a test. When they compare themselves to the prodigals, they figure they are doing pretty well. When they compare themselves to other performers, they fear that they are inferior. They strive for perfection in every endeavor and are, as a result, usually worn out, anxious, and unhappy. Because they imagine that love and approval are based upon performance, they fear that they can lose their parents' good opinion, and by extension, their place in their parents' hearts and home.

Chapter 9

Becoming Socrates:
My Homeschool Education

> "He, O men, is the wisest, who, like Socrates, knows that his wisdom is in truth worth nothing." [1]
>
> "Because you say, 'I am rich, have become wealthy, and have need of nothing'—and do not know that you are wretched, miserable, poor, blind, and naked—I counsel you to buy from Me gold refined in the fire, that you may be rich; and white garments, that you may be clothed, that the shame of your nakedness may not be revealed; and anoint your eyes with eye salve, that you may see" (Revelation 3:17-18).

At the end of the day, I am pretty sure I learned more from my homeschooling experience than I taught. For starters, my educational philosophy has undergone dramatic changes. Whereas initially I worked toward mastery learning with the understanding that education

---

1. Plato, *The Apology*, trans. Benjamin Jowett (November 3, 2008), www.gutenberg.org/files/1656/1656-h/1656-h.htm.

was all about getting the right answers and passing a test, I have come to define education as the acquisition of wisdom. It is true that the applications of these two philosophies look very similar on the surface: both involve reading a lot of books, discussing their contents, memorizing and analyzing data, and taking tests. Yet these activities are directed toward different ends when pursued in the shadow of these paradigms.

In a mastery learning environment, school activities produce two types of kids: successes and failures. Far from presenting the real world's untamed grandeur, mystery, beauty, and terror, and inviting kids to discover their place within it, mastery education presents a reductionist para-world to be subjugated. This subtly elevates those who succeed to the status of miniature gods, superior to others and so, like Flannery O'Connor's Mr. Head, suitable to lead. Students learn to measure their success and form their sense of identity from their grades.

For the performers (the Cans), school becomes an arena in which to validate themselves. The more success they garner, the more prone they are to fall into pride and egotism. For the non-performers (the Can'ts) school often becomes odious. They know subconsciously that their successful peers are not quantitatively different from them, and they come to resent their honors. Often, they feel sorry for themselves, considering that they were not born with equal advantages. Others become scornful, disdaining school altogether. They learn to hate the system that brands winners and losers by measure of the grade. Like their peers, they become arrogant, rejecting any knowledge that portrays them to the world and to themselves as failures.

Conversely, the pursuit of wisdom looks a lot more like humility than godhood. This project can get a little messy, since wisdom requires gaining a new sight of self in view of God and others, but its benefits are virtually limitless. For example, the academic disciplines, rather than representing opportunities to convince students they are the masters of the world and captains of their souls, instead represent opportunities to intrude on each student's kingdom of self.

As they study science, they discover that there is a world that exists outside of them, that was before them, and that will remain after them. They find that the hard realities of this world require their respect and recognition. They learn that there is an order which they themselves did not establish, a cosmic unity that they do not maintain. They are pressed by the weight of all there is to know and are led to discover their own limitations. With this respect for the sheer magnitude of the world in which they live, they develop a sense of wonder and curiosity.

As they study history, they find that others came before them and intuit that more will come after them. As their world becomes larger, they become smaller. They discover the things for which their forebears lived and died, and in the recorded pursuits of these dead men, they find a reflection of their own desires that invites contemplation. Not only do they become familiar with natural consequences, but they discover the timelessness of human nature. In their study of literature, they encounter goodness, justice, truth, and beauty. They rejoice when goodness is rewarded and when evil is punished. They cry when a good man falls. They discover that truth is objective. They survey the questions that other men have posed regarding the nature of the world and man. They are pressed to ask those questions themselves, and in the questioning, they discover their creaturehood. They develop empathy.

Presented with an intelligently designed universe and rational man, they discover that there remains work to be done in this world. Inspired by the historic contributions of others, they aspire to make their own contribution. Confronted with their limitations, they are forced to develop character in the pursuit of their goals.

By means of the education for wisdom paradigm, students learn through the academic disciplines to know themselves and their neighbors. The ancient Greek philosopher Socrates taught, in accordance with the Delphic inscription, "Know thyself." He believed that familiarity with the self was the source of wisdom, and that further wisdom was impossible without it. True self-knowledge is a game changer. Whereas mastery learning tends to produce answer men, wisdom produces humility, empathy, and an appreciation for others.

In order to lead children into this kind of wisdom, educators are forced to contemplate such things themselves. Rather than posing as repositories of all knowledge, teachers are constrained to become co-learners, modeling humility and wonder. In order to successfully lead children into wisdom, we must ourselves become wise enough to assume the posture of a child and learner. This alone changes the nature of the homeschool environment. Learning becomes a shared pursuit, and the self-knowledge it yields produces fellowship.

Of course, this is all educational philosophy. How does it work in real life? In my experience, twenty years of homeschooling taught me that I will not master all knowledge. There will always be books I have not read, history I have not encountered, math I cannot figure, scientific facts that are too big for my limited mind to comprehend. What is more, it has convinced me that my children will never master it all either. I have realized that children are not muffins to be baked by following a recipe perfectly. They are not, after all, the works of our own hands, but ongoing, creative works of God.

With my kids, I have discovered that my failures are often more fruitful than my successes. I have recognized my bent toward self-glorification and felt the consequences of this in my relationships with them and with my peers. I have been driven to the realization that every impulse and motivation of my heart, even the best ones, are infected with original sin, and from this posture I have been forced to admit my ongoing deficit and need for a Savior.

Simultaneously, the children have witnessed God's grace working in my life and have experienced real changes both in our daily homeschooling and our relationships with each other. Where once a desire to prove and preserve myself influenced our homeschool activities, now Christianity informs my pursuit of wisdom, supplying the answers to the whys of my condition.

The visceral data suggests that I am no master, but a subject, mouthing the name of the true Master. The common instances of grace I have experienced, in the face of my own hubris, have become indications, demonstrations of this Master's true nature and goodness. The benefits I have received have become felt blessings. The struggles I have endured make me aware of the struggles of my children and neighbors, and a new grace informs my relationships with them. Learning has become a lifetime pursuit to know God and experience His goodness, to discover in new ways His kindness, mercy, and love.

We in the homeschool movement consider our students the next, best hope for the redemption of the culture, and we say that we want to glorify God in our work with them. I think we deceive ourselves when we believe that we accomplish this by making ourselves and our students more perfect.

What, exactly, is it that glorifies God? When is His nature and goodness most visible? Is it not when we call on Him, depend on Him, receive from Him? The Old Testament prophet Isaiah expressed this when he wrote: "When You make His soul an offering for sin, He shall see His seed, He shall prolong His days, and the pleasure of the Lord shall prosper in His hand. He shall see the travail of His soul and be satisfied. By His knowledge My righteous Servant shall justify many, For He shall bear their iniquities" (Isaiah 53:10b-11). In our weakness, Jesus' strength is magnified. "For He said unto me: My grace is sufficient for thee, for my strength is made perfect in weakness" (2 Corinthians 12:9). Doesn't glorifying God mean humbling ourselves to recognize and repent of our sins and receive His righteousness?

We opine about raising up kingdom-extenders for the glory of God. I have come through my own experience to see this very differently than I once did. I have discovered that I cannot change the world. I cannot change my neighbor. I cannot even really change myself. And yet, this revelation has not discouraged me. Rather, through it I can see that I myself am being changed. Not a master of the kingdom, I have instead become a subject, the object of divine love and the work of God's hands. Having abandoned my efforts to be a god, I find that I am being changed by the only God, and as a result, His kingdom is extended in me. Sharing His grace has become my new paradigm of kingdom building.

God's kingdom does not look like the kingdoms of this world, which run on the strength of men and minds. Rather His is a kingdom, as theologian Robert Capon explains it, of "the little, the lost and the least:"

> *'Follow me,' [Jesus] says flatly. 'Follow me into my death, because it is only in my death and resurrection that the kingdom comes. All the other tickets to the final, reconciled party – all the moral, philosophical, and religious admission slips on which humanity has always counted – have been cancelled. Nothing counts*

now except being last, least, lost, little, and dead with me. Buy that, and you're home free; buy anything else and you're out in the cold.' [2]

As I live with my children in the communion of creaturehood, need, and grace, I become a witness to the work of our Master. God is the world-changer, and He is changing us into the image of Christ, not by our good performances or our diligent duties, but by His persistent paradigm of death and resurrection.

Homeschooling is a fine arena in which to experience this death and resurrection. Through home education, the Lord is raising up a new generation, but not a generation of sinless saints and powerbrokers. Rather, He is raising up a generation of believers who know themselves to be objects of Divine affection and who revel in the identity they have received from their Father. He is raising up the lost, the least, and the last, not to change the world, but to enjoy it, not to usher in the kingdom, but to receive it. As recipients of grace, we traffic in this new economy, extending to others what we have ourselves received.

For parent teachers who labor in this arena, the encouragement the Lord gave to Paul resonates: "My grace is sufficient for thee: for my strength is made perfect in weakness." This allows us to maintain with Paul, "Most gladly therefore will I rather glory in my infirmities, that the power of Christ may rest upon me. Therefore I take

---

2. Robert Farrar Capon, *Grace, Judgment: Paradox, Outrage, and Vindication in the Parables of Jesus* (Grand Rapids: Eerdmans, 2002), 205.

pleasure in infirmities, in reproaches, in necessities, in persecutions, in distresses for Christ's sake: for when I am weak, then am I strong" (2 Corinthians 12:9-10). Our weaknesses protect us from overweening pride and deceitful ambition and protect our children from confusing us (and subsequently themselves) with God. As they witness our struggles and experience their own, they are delivered from their idolatry of self and pointed to the God who loves them. In this way, their weakness (yes, and even their sin) occasions a demonstration of the mercy and love of the only, wise God.

Through His adverse work, what Robert Capon calls His "left-handed power," God will continue His good work of redeeming the world, one individual at a time.[3]

---

[3]. The adverse work of God signifies the apparently negative circumstances God sovereignly allows into the lives of His children for their advantage. While these things appear evil, they are meant for good. Consider the words of the patriarch Joseph when speaking to his alienated brothers, years after they had sinned against him by selling him into slavery in Egypt: "But as for you, you meant evil against me; but God meant it for good, in order to bring it about as it is this day, to save many people alive" (Genesis 50:20). Strangers were not the only ones to be saved through Joseph's trials, but Joseph himself was changed. Robert Capon calls this type of power God's left-handed power. He explains that right-handed power, or interventionism, is a show of strength and action, while its counterpart is a more passive (albeit undiminished) power or work in the believer's life. The cross itself is a demonstration of this left-handed power, suggesting that the strength and efficacy of this type of power is in no way inferior to its more commonly understood, muscular counterpart. While the Jews of Jesus' time expected a Messiah that would strong arm the Roman authorities, Jesus took a left-handed approach to the kingdom problem: He died. The effects of His sacrifice continue to change the world.

This He will effect, as He has ever done, through His mysterious work on the cross, through substitutionary atonement, self-sacrificial love, and imputed righteousness. The good news is that this work, albeit ongoing in our individual lives and the lives of our children, is ultimately a *fait accompli*. Jesus implied this by His final words upon the cross: "It is finished." The jury is in, and the verdict on us and our children is a resounding "not guilty."

Not only has Jesus's "my life for yours" work delivered us from judgment, it has also earned us the validation and honor of sonship. Having been baptized into the death of Christ, we live His resurrected life. "For me to live is Christ, to die is gain" (Philippians 1:21). We receive the validation of the Son, through imputation, and hear with Him the Father's voice, "This is my beloved Son, in whom I am well pleased." Freed thus from our frantic chase for validation, we can rest in His love. Recipients of the family identity and the Father's love, we can labor at the work of our hands from a position of acceptance, rather than for one. Our work, in this way, becomes a joyful activity, rather than a ceaseless identity quest.

Having discovered that we are beloved children of a good Father, we become fit instruments for His continued work of redeeming the world. Having gained hearts of wisdom, we are uniquely prepared to experience our *raison d'être*, expressed so succinctly by the words of the Westminster Catechism, "to glorify God, and to enjoy

Him forever."[4] This is the end goal of education. This is the end goal of life. In this alone will we find rest, peace, identity, validation, belonging, meaning, and fulfillment. Everything else represents a mere chasing of our own tails.

Having seen ourselves in this way, we will at last be fit for relationship with others. Our experience in community will emerge as a joyful byproduct of our own redemption, a shared celebration of belonging and provision. In this way, our gifts will be made useful to others. Rather than the means to identity, we will discover our talents to be God's good provision for His body; we will become the gifts of God to one another. No longer shall we reject the gifts and abilities of others because they annihilate our own sense of selves, but instead we shall receive one another, honor one another, bless one another, enjoy one another.

In this world of the now and the not yet, we may in this way experience a foretaste of eternity. Although our sin nature remains, it functions as an ever-present insurance policy against our own ambition, a constant signpost directing us home. For we have a home, a place secure in God's family, just as our children have a home in this world with us independent of their decisions, their activities, or their successes. In the Father's home school, we are all lifetime learners, and every discipline reveals His glory and love.

---

4. G.I. Williamson, *The Shorter Catechism, Volume 1* (Phillipsburg, NJ: Presbyterian and Reformed Publishing Co., 1970), 1.

Chapter 10

Little Onions and New Wine: The Banquet of the Suffering

> "'We are rejoicing,' the little, thin old man went on. 'We are drinking the new wine, the wine of new, great gladness; do you see how many guests? Here are the bride and bridegroom, here is the wise governor of the feast, he is tasting the new wine. Why do you wonder at me? I gave an onion to a beggar, so I, too, am here. And many here have given only an onion each—only one little onion... What are all our deeds? And you, my gentle one, you, my kind boy, you too have known how to give a famished woman an onion to-day. Begin your work, dear one... Do you see our Sun, do you see Him?'"[1]

It is tempting when suffering to assume that we are different than our neighbors and that our experiences are unique in the world. The Bible tells us differently: "No temptation has overtaken you except what is common to mankind" (1 Corinthians 10:13a). Although our sins take the shape of our own personalities, they retain the

---

1. Dostoevsky, *The Brothers Karamazov*, 199.

common denominator of humanity.

When we believe our sins are unique among men, we alienate ourselves from the larger community. Of course, it is easy to see why we do this. Few are willing to share the deep secrets of their sinful hearts. It's scary. It's risky. It's uncertain. If others knew who we really were, they would surely reject us, right? Wrong. When we get brave enough to share the reality of ourselves with others, we discover that what we most have in common is our sin and need for grace.

1 John puts it this way: "If we claim to have fellowship with [God] and yet walk in darkness, we lie and do not live out the truth. But if we walk in the light, as He is in the light, we have fellowship with one another, and the blood of Jesus, His Son, purifies us from all sin." Walking in the light, that act of telling the truth about ourselves, sin and all, produces a profound fellowship that corporately salves the wound of human experience with the atoning blood of Jesus. As the body of Christ, we have the honor of extending to others the grace by which we ourselves were saved. When we do, we experience the joy of salvation all over again. Relationships spring up, the real kind with no masks, no "glittering images"[2] involved. When we deliver to others the grace that was granted to us, we become the salt of the earth Jesus mentions in Matthew 5:13.

Russian author Fyodor Dostoevsky characterizes this response to grace as "the giving of an onion," the savor

---

2. Manning, Brennan, *Abba's Child: The Cry of the Heart for Intimate Belonging* (Colorado Springs, CO: Navpress, 2002), 25.

in the human experience. By way of illustration, he tells a Russian folk tale about a peasant woman who dies and finds herself damned to the lake of fire. Suffering terribly, she begs her guardian angel to pull her out. He petitions the Lord for permission and is permitted that, if the woman has ever demonstrated any goodness or faith, then he might "extend an onion" to her and drag her out of the fiery lake. Probing through her past, the angel lights on one small, but momentous act of humanity. He extends the onion. As he begins to pull the woman out, other damned souls in the lake moan and beg her to take them with her, but the woman viciously beats them away. In the struggle, the onion breaks, and she is left in the lake with the rest. None are saved. Dostoevsky remarks that the woman's unwillingness to extend empathy to her neighbors results in death for everyone. Quaint and strange though it be, this folktale suggests the truth that graceless living destroys both the individual and the community.

Alternatively, Dostoevsky creates a hero, the aspiring churchman Alyosha, who discovers the joy of fellowship when he empathizes with the lowly. In a particularly moving scene, Alyosha guilelessly extends kindness to a fallen woman even as she attempts to corrupt him. Without judgment, he identifies with her depravity, calling her "sister." This unmerited generosity deeply affects her: "Hush, Alyosha, your words make me ashamed, for I am bad and not good – that's what I am...I shall begin to cry, I shall...He called me his sister and I shall never forget that." [3] By his simple willingness to walk in the light, Alyosha wrings humanity and repentance from the woman, and she is forever changed.

It is easy to believe that the "onion" in Dostoevsky's folk tale represents some good work, but the author disabuses readers of this notion. The revered Father Zossima, the novel's spiritual compass, terms the deed Alyosha's first act of empathy: "And you, my gentle one, you, my kind boy, you too have known how to give a famished woman an onion to-day."[4] Alyosha merely identified with the woman in his humanity, exposing his vulnerability and need. In turn, she is so profoundly altered that readers recognize the scene as a marked conversion experience in her life.

Like the Apostle John, Dostoevsky understood that graceful living produces fellowship. What is more, he understood that this ability to identify with the sinful proceeds directly from Christ's willingness to identify with man. In His role as Redeemer, Christ's most profound work was identifying with humanity in His suffering. Of course, Christ's suffering, unlike ours, was undeserved. The only sinless human being that ever lived, His affliction was the result of our sin. "For our sake, [God] made Him to be sin who knew no sin, so that in Him we might become the righteousness of God" (2 Corinthians 5:21). Jesus' willingness to assume human flesh and bear human burdens, to call us, as Dostoevsky called the woman, brothers and sisters and to live transparently

---

3. Dostoevsky, *The Brothers Karamazov*, 193.
4. Dostoevsky, *The Brothers Karamazov*, 199.

with us, produced a community, a family in which we all have place. From that sure place, we are encouraged to begin our own work of identification, not despising our membership in sinful humanity, but owning it with the knowledge that our neediness is what makes our membership certain. "I did not come to call the righteous, but sinners, to repentance" (Mark 2:17). Dostoevsky's novel implies that this "work" of extending empathy and grace is the good work that characterizes true members of the family of God.

Far from a work of the flesh, this "good work" of empathy rests necessarily on faith in Christ's righteous atonement. Only one convinced of the imputed perfection of Christ can afford to countenance his own imperfections, let alone admit them to others. Ultimately, the foundation of fellowship with God lies in the New Wine of the Gospel of Grace. True fellowship with other men flows from this relationship experientially, creating a derivative conviviality in the body of Christ.

The term New Wine refers to the New Covenant, written, figuratively speaking, in the shed blood of Jesus Christ. Whereas the Old Covenant required the perfect performance of the Law by those who would be justified by it, the New Covenant finds satisfaction exclusively in the perfect performance of Christ Jesus: His sinless life, undeserved death, and ultimate resurrection. The New Covenant is the Gospel of God's grace. Jesus Himself likened the gospel of the New Covenant to New Wine in Mark 2:22: "No one puts new wine into old wine skins; or else the new wine bursts the wineskins and the wine is spilled…" Just as new wine requires new wine skins, the New Covenant required the end of the Jewish system (the old container of the Spirit) and the beginning of a new way of relating to God.

The metaphor of new wine plays nicely with the first miracle of Jesus at the wedding at Cana, when He turned water into a wine that surpassed the needs of the moment with astounding superiority of quality and quantity, thereby demonstrating the divine graciousness that would abound in His fulfillment of the terms of the Old Covenant for the transformative benefit of man.

Dostoevsky references this allegorical interpretation of the first miracle in *The Brothers Karamazov* when Alyosha dreams of the wedding at Cana. That this miraculous gospel was enacted to ensure the joy of the poor informs not only Alyosha's perception of the miracle, but his understanding of the meaning of suffering and the mission of man. Through inference, he notes that Jesus redeems mankind by identification in suffering; likewise, the Savior invites man to participate in His sufferings, identifying with Him in His crucifixion. Those who do, he suggests, become living vessels of the New Wine of the gospel for other thirsty sinners. Like the water Jesus turned into wine, their suffering, poured out for others, results in fellowship and joy.

This is why I pour out the story of my sin to you. I share so that you will know that you are not alone. I share because I identify with the sinful struggles inherent in homeschooling and mothering. I know the distress, the discouragement, the overwork, and the exhaustion endemic to this career. I understand a mother's peculiar proclivity to conflate her children's successes with her own, their merit with hers, thereby muddying the altruistic waters of the childrearing project with ugly, derivative self-interestedness. I have experienced it myself. I empathize. I extend to you my little onion and the wine of the New Covenant. Let's feast together on the Master's miraculous grace.

Chapter 11

Glorious Grace: The Great Game Changer

> *"She said, 'I think I like your soul the way it is.'*
> *He looked at her and laughed, and his color rose."*[1]

It is only in authentic relationships that we are receptive to love. When our masks are carefully in place, we may easily discount the love given to us, mistaking it as payment for services rendered. We assume the mask accrues it, and not our true selves. Steve Brown of Key Life Ministries speaks to this in his book *Hidden Agendas*:

> *We live in a reward-based culture. Do it right and it will come out right. Other than the fact that it's not true, it really does sound good. After all, if we studied*

---

[1]. Marilynne Robinson, *Home* (New York: Farrar, Strauss and Giroux, 2008), 105.

hard, we got good grades. If we worked hard, we got a promotion. If we were nice, people were nice to us… So we work hard, live pure, and are nice. When it turns out that we can't work that hard, live that pure, or be that nice, we create a mask. The mask reflects our shame and the horrible fear that others will see. Then we become 'islands' unto ourselves, lonely, fearful, and guilty. But what if we said, "I'm not playing that game anymore, even if nothing turns out right?" Let me tell you what would happen: love would happen. We would discover that God hugs dirty kids. Then love would happen to us from God and from us to others. It wouldn't be the phony love that is given in response to being good, pure, successful, nice, and strong. That's not love; that's reward. In fact, you can't know love until you know you don't deserve it. In other words, you can't know love until you are willing to risk getting it by taking off the mask.[2]

When we live in the open, love is grace and everyone knows it. This is a cause for rejoicing! By grace we become members of a new society whose currency differs from the economics of the common world. Grace is its species, and its peculiar property is that no matter how much of it we spend, it continually abounds: "And God is able to make all grace abound toward you, that you, always having all sufficiency in all things, may have an abundance for every good work" (2 Corinthians 9:8). This abundance of grace makes us fit for the good work

---

2. Steve Brown, *Hidden Agendas [Dropping the Masks That Keep Us Apart]* (Greensboro,: New Growth Press, 2016), 18-19.

of the kingdom.

Without this understanding of unmerited love, our perception of place and pursuit of love will inevitably be linked with our performance. Responses to this economy of merit range widely and include striving, rebelling, and despairing. Each of these responses grows out of the same fundamental misperception: we are what we do. Function is identity. This presupposition bears a variety of fruits, none of them peace.

Marilynne Robinson contemplates such results in her novel, *Home*, which depicts the life and relationships of an aging pastor and his adult children. Robinson features two of these children in her story. The protagonist and narrator of the story is Glory, Rev. Boughton's middle-aged daughter, who finds herself living at home and taking care of her aging father after a foray into the world leaves her alone, disappointed, and disillusioned. She is joined by her brother Jack, the prodigal who always knew he wouldn't measure up to the role of the virtuous son, and so sped his way to ruin in self-fulfilling prophecy. Each child measures success through their father's ethical and religious teaching. Each experiences disillusionment and isolation. When the loneliness and estrangement overwhelm Jack, he attempts suicide. Glory finds him:

> *She put the keys in her pocket and walked out to the barn. She opened the door and stepped into the humid half-darkness. And there he was, propped against the car, with the brim of his hat bent down, holding his la-*

pels closed with one hand. He held the other out to her, discreetly, just at the level of his waist, and said, "Spare a dime, lady?" He was smiling, a look of raffish, haggard charm, hard, humiliated charm, that stunned her. "It's your brother Jack," he said. "Your brother Jack without his disguise." [3]

Living together in close quarters strips all three family members of their disguises, and they are each forced to see themselves more clearly than they had before. Yet self-pity dims this sight.

In a long conversation with his children, Papa Boughton speaks: "Maybe I'm finding out I'm not such a good man as I thought I was. Now that I don't have the strength—patience takes a lot out of you. Hope, too."[4] (274). Although Boughton has begun to see himself, his self-pity blinds him to the accusation that freights his confession. This strikes home in his son's heart, confirming the identity he assumes: Disappointment, Failure, No Good.

As a result of this relationship with their father, home, for Jack and Glory, is a mixed bag; the blessings of the past make their present failures heavier and more shameful to them. Glory explains: "Home. What kinder place could there be on earth, and why did it seem to them all like exile?... But the soul finds its own home if it ever has a home at all." [5] The expectations of the

---

3. Robinson, *Home*, 243.
4. Ibid., 274.
5. Ibid., 282.

Boughton household clothe the children with an identity predicated upon their behavior, and they wear it for life. Going home makes such suits wear like iron.

For the performer, the confusion of *doing* with *being* means a lifetime on the treadmill. He does well, but to keep a good record, he must never stop achieving, always keep doing. Nick Lannon of Mockingbird Ministries explains that the performance-based life is a lot like the high jump event of track and field competitions. No one ever really wins in the high jump because the bar is always being raised. It's only a matter of time before you just can't get over it. Failure is always just around the corner. Winning, then, just means jumping higher than your neighbor. A performer never really rests in his or her identity because the bar of performance expectation just keeps going up. The law demands perfect obedience, but perfection belongs to God alone. If perfection is required, then our petty performance only serves to damn us.

For the rebel, this confusion provokes her to give up before she starts. This may look like rejecting the law and performance forcefully as something only for "losers" and "prigs," or it may take the shape of the depressed underachiever, the "Can't" in the corner. Each of these personalities, like their performer counterpart, considers her identity in relationship to her performance, according to her relationship to the law. The rebel says, *I am the one who won't perform. I am the one who rejects the law*. The underachiever moans in self-pity, *I am the one who fails to keep the law*. Both personalities are just the flip sides of the shiny coin of performancism.

In the final analysis, however, we are not what we do at all. By God's gracious proclamation, we receive our identities: "Beloved." By Jesus' gracious act of redemption, He justifies us. We are what the Lord has done: "We are His workmanship, created in Christ Jesus for good works which God prepared beforehand that we should walk in them" (Ephesians 2:10). Our actions, our good works, are born out of the personhood God gave us when He created and redeemed us. He has made us, and not our own actions. He is the Lord. All things derive their identity from Him; we are no exception.

Identity is not self-created, but rather discovered. Consider Adam's work of naming the animals in the garden. Far from an act of creation, his work involved recognizing what God had already made. In the process, he discovered much about himself, too.

When we look to the Lord, we find that His Word tells us everything we need to know about ourselves. There we discover our moral deficiencies: "There is none righteous, no not one" (Romans 3:10). We discover our uniqueness among creation: "He has made them a little lower than the angels and crowned them with glory and honor" (Psalm 8:5). We discover our grandeur: "So God created mankind in his own image, in the image of God he created them; male and female he created them" (Genesis 1:27). We discover our belovedness: "God so loved the world that He gave His only begotten Son, that whosoever believes in Him should not perish, but have eternal life" (John 3:16). We discover our family name:

"Yet to all who receive him, to those who believed in His name, he gave the right to become children of God" (John 1:12). "'I will be a Father to you, and you will be my sons and daughters,' says the Lord Almighty" (2 Corinthians 6:18). We discover our purpose: "But you are a chosen people, a royal priesthood, a holy nation, God's special possession, that you may declare the praises of him who called you out of darkness into his wonderful light" (1 Peter 2:9). In God's Word, we discover our true identities, which are based not on our doing, but on our Maker's wonderful work. He created us (Genesis 1:27). He calls us (Romans 8:30). He redeems us (Titus 2:14). He prepares the very work that we will do (Ephesians 2:10). He keeps us as the apple of His eye (Zechariah 2:8). We are His special treasure (Deuteronomy 7:6).

If we were to grab hold of this defining reality, the performers among us would cease to regard their activities with pride or fear. The under-achievers would stop feeling envious and sorry for themselves. The rebels would put down their fists. Everyone would smile. Our doings would stop being the stuff of our heavenly resumes, the things we present to God for acceptability and place. Instead they would become what they were always meant to be: the inevitable fruits of our belovedness in Christ.

The closest thing Robinson's Jack experiences to this in *Home* comes from his sister and fellow failure, aptly named Glory. In a conversation with her about the eternal things, she extends this belovedness, giving him a name and a home. Jack begins:

> "... I think it is usual to ponder great truths. That has been my experience."
>
> "Such as?"
>
> "The fatherhood of God, for one. The idea being that the splendor of creation and of the human creature testify to a gracious intention lying behind it all, that they manifest divine mercy and love. Which sustains the world in general and is present in the experience of, you know, people whose souls are saved. Or will be.... I always nourish the suspicion that pious folk are plotting my rescue..."
>
> She said, "I think I like your soul the way it is." [6]

Glory lives up to her name when she extends love and family membership to her brother. Her willingness to love Jack as he is is an image of glory. This manifestation of divine mercy and love, as Jack puts it, does indeed sustain and save the world.

Imagine what a life oriented by this truth would look like in a homeschool environment. Rather than a job by which parents must prove their mettle, homeschooling would become an opportunity to model the posture of learners, to walk in humility, wonder, repentance, and

---

6. Robinson, *Home*, 104-105.

forgiveness with one's children according to the New Testament economy of grace. In this environment, children could admit their ignorance and begin to learn, free from fears of failure. Families would grow, rooted in the gospel of Christ.

Imagine the effect of this truth in a homeschool co-op. Released from the baggage of performance, parents could admit their personal deficiencies and needs to one another without feeling shame or inferiority, receiving help from those whose personal gifts and interests meet those needs. Liberated from idolatry, the body could minister to itself with every joint supplying, even as the Apostle Paul suggests in his letter to the Ephesians:

> *And He Himself gave some to be apostles, some prophets, some evangelists, and some pastors and teachers, for the equipping of the saints for the work of the ministry, for the edifying of the body of Christ, till we all come to the unity of the faith and the knowledge of the Son of God, to a perfect man, to the measure of the stature of the fullness of Christ; that we should no longer be children tossed to and fro and carried about with every wind of doctrine, by the trickery of men, in the cunning craftiness by which they lie in wait to deceive, but, speaking the truth in love, may grow up in all things into Him who is the head – Christ – from whom the whole body, joined and knit together by what every joint supplies, according to the effective working by which every part does its share, causes growth of the body for the edifying of itself in love.* (Ephesians

4:12-16)

The peculiar gifts given to individuals are not given to make much of their possessors, but rather are given to meet the needs of the community. The people themselves are God's gifts to His body. Furthermore, this intricate exchange of needs and surplus knit the body of Christ together in love and unity (2 Corinthians 8:15). Performance cultures, however, obscure this provision of God for His children.

What would happen if we really believed that our identity in the family of God was grounded in sonship? How might this change our understanding of individual gifts and abilities? Your ten-talent neighbor would cease to be a pain in your side, showing you up by running energetic circles around you, and would become instead a personal blessing to you. Likewise, the inactivity and restfulness of the "little ones" in the congregation would serve as visible, healthful reminders of the terms of body membership: not performance, but belovedness.

How might this understanding of value and identity affect the workplace? How might it affect the world? The ramifications of this gospel are too far reaching to list. It is truly good news. The believer's identity in Christ is the source of all peace and a fountain of rest. It changes everything.

Chapter 12

The Fortunate Fall: A Paradox of Severe Mercy

> *"For God judged it better to bring good out of evil than not to permit any evil to exist."* [1]

Whenever I tell my homeschool story, my listeners always seem to ask the same question: How can I avoid this? They want to know what they can do to keep themselves from using their children to establish or support their own identities, how they can avoid the consequences that follow this sin for their own sake and for the sake of their children. What should you do if you have seen yourself in my story? How do you fix a homeschool day gone bad, or a year, or a career for that matter?

I have already alluded to the fact that it is relatively

---

1. Aurelius Augustine, *Enchiridion on Faith, Hope, and Love*, ed. Albert C. Outler, Ph.D., D.D. Perkins School of Theology (1955), www.tertullian.org/fathers/augustine_enchiridion_02_trans.htm.

The Fortunate Fall

useless to try to avoid scenarios like the ones I have described. Trying to avoid mistakes in your homeschooling and parenting is like trying to avoid being human. Subject to finitude, we cannot see tomorrow, let alone next year, and seeing ourselves, well, that is even harder!

While striving for perfection and obedience is noble, it remains futile. No matter how resolutely we address our weaknesses and failures, intending to do the good and improve, we inevitably find ourselves returning like dogs to our own vomit (Proverbs 26:11). Like the Apostle Paul, we mutter in confusion: "I do not understand what I do. For what I want to do I do not do, but what I hate I do...For I know that in me (that is, in my flesh) nothing good dwells: for to will is present with me, but how to perform what is good I do not find" (Romans 7:15-17). Knowing the good does not empower us to do the good. Our trouble, Paul suggests, is not an information problem, but a sin problem, and so we cry with him: "O wretched man that I am! Who will deliver me from this body of death? I thank God – through Jesus Christ our Lord!" (Romans 7:24-25a). Help comes from the outside, from Jesus, our Rescue.

When the Law, performing its proper function, exposes our sin, we would do better to respond by abandoning our attempts at righteousness and clinging to Christ's than by renewing our resolution to improve. If you see yourself in my story, then the first thing you should do is repent! The Law reveals the nature and will of the perfect God of the universe, and we see ourselves better by contrast. Fallen creatures, we are not gods, but stand in need of Him. Repent, and ask God for His forgiveness and righteousness. Once you've done this, it's time to repent to your kids, too. Tell them what you've seen of yourself and the wisdom it has produced. Ask them for forgiveness. You might be surprised by their response.

Our sin would be infinitely bad news if divine revelation had not likewise revealed God's love for and commitment to man. Yet in the incarnation and life of Christ, in His death and resurrection, the upright God of the universe condescended to do for man what man could not do for himself. In Jesus, we find the righteousness that the Law through judgment could not produce in us. Faced with our shortfall, therefore, rather than positing new resolutions to try harder and do better, we do best to trust in God – His perfect work and magnificent revelation of Himself in Christ. Look to Him daily for grace as you humbly confess your sin and failings, and watch Him transform you and your home into a place of peace and rest. Know too that in this you are modeling repentance for your children. This might be the most important lesson they ever learn from you.

Not finite, but omniscient, God sees the end from the beginning. While we make ourselves completely paranoid trying unsuccessfully to avoid every misstep, God has promised not only to guide our steps, but also to make all things work together for good in our lives: "And we know that all things work together for good to them that love God, to them who are the called according to His purpose" (Romans 8:28). "All things" really does mean all. Paul is not just addressing those things that befall man, which remain outside of human control. He addresses all things, including a man's sin and errors. Even sin, it seems, is not beyond the omnipotent sovereignty of our loving Lord. This is good news! In fact, this idea resonates with Augustine's doctrine of the Fortunate Fall: "For God judged it better to bring good out of evil than not to permit any evil to exist." Augustine suggests that the Fall of Man in the garden was not an accident, the sending of Jesus to atone for man's sin not some divine Plan B. Rather, he asserts that the Fall, in a sense, occasioned man's education. For by it, man simultaneously came to know both his own insufficiency and God's perfect love.

Seventeenth century poet John Milton, author of the English epic *Paradise Lost*, concurs. In his verse, he reimagines the Fall. He depicts God seated in heaven, surveying his newly created earth and watching the vanquished rebel: "Satan there / Coasting the wall of Heav'n on this side Night / In the dun Air sublime, and ready now / To stoop with wearied wings, and willing feet / On the bare outside of this World..." [2] From this vantage, God predicts man's Fall, proclaiming it inspired by Satan, but naming the fault man's: "For Man will heark'n to his glozing lies, / And easily transgress the sole Command, / Sole pledge of his obedience: So will fall / He and his faithless Progeny: whose fault? /

---

2. John Milton, *Paradise Lost* in *The Great Books of the Western World Vol. 29* (Chicago: Encyclopaedia Britannica, 1990), 3.80-96.

Whose but his own?" [3] (Paradise Lost 3.80-96).

Yet Milton's God foreshadows His master plan to His Son and the full company of heavenly host that attend Him: "Man therefore shall find grace…in Mercy and Justice both, / Through Heav'n and Earth, so shall my glory excel, / But Mercy first and last shall brightest shine." [4] Through the fall, Milton suggests, man would come to know himself and God in a way that would have proven impossible otherwise. He would come to understand the magnificent love and grace of his Creator as he received it undeservedly. Similarly, the failures in our lives occasion personal encounters with God. These become opportunities for us to know Him better in His love, power, and redemptive mercy, and likewise to know ourselves better as objects of His special affection.

Not only do our failures put us in the way of a relationship with God, but they also position us for better relationships with one another. As we noted in the previous chapter, the same way that the variable excess and want in the body of Christ creates unity, the failures that create sin-deficits in our relationships with others, necessitating a superflux of forgiveness that can only be obtained through divine intervention, knit us together in mutual vulnerability. Grace becomes the theme of the day, and Christ, its author and source, is glorified.
I can hear objections even now; such came to the Apostle Paul, too. "What then? shall we sin, because we are not under the law, but under grace?" (Romans 6:15).

---

3. Ibid.,3.80-96.
4. Ibid., 3.125-135

The Fortunate Fall

My answer resonates with his: "God forbid" (Romans 6:15b). Certainly, I am not advocating a flippant lack of gravity or an intentional and profligate run toward sin by homeschool parents. I merely recognize that in this life, the Christian remains what Reformation theologian Martin Luther called *simul justus et peccator*, or in English "simultaneously saint and sinner." [5]

How are we to live with the knowledge that sin breeds death when our own best efforts to keep the law and avoid sin produce in us the very thing we wish to avoid? Who shall deliver us from these bodies of death?! (Romans 7:24) The answer to our predicament is embodied in the gracious gospel of Jesus Christ: His perfect life, His undeserved, substitutionary, atoning death, and His glorious resurrection. This gospel promises not only to redeem our physical bodies at the end of time, but likewise to redeem our daily lives here and now.

The Gospel of Jesus Christ is like the "Deeper Magic Before the Dawn of Time" that C. S. Lewis describes in his children's classic, *The Lion, the Witch, and the Wardrobe*. In the story, Edmund, a type of Adam, is enslaved by the White Witch, a usurper in the country created and ruled by Aslan. For his treason, his life is forfeit. Yet, Aslan returns and brokers a deal with the witch, offering his life in exchange for Edmund's. The children watch from hiding as their enemy snuffs the life out of the hero they looked to for rescue. Yet, before their eyes

---

5. Martin Luther, "Preface to Romans" from *Lectures on Romans*, messiah'skingdom.com, www.messiahs_kingdom.com/resources/The-Gospel/luther-romans.pdf.

were dry from weeping, there was a magnificent crack, and the stone table upon which the witch had executed the lion-king split from top to bottom:

> "Who's done it?" cried Susan. "What does it mean? Is it more magic?"...
> "It means," said Aslan, "that though the Witch knew the Deep Magic, there is a magic deeper still which she did not know. Her knowledge goes back only to the dawn of time. But if she could have looked a little further back, into the stillness and the darkness before Time dawned, she would have read there a different incantation. She would have known that when a willing victim who had committed no treachery was killed in a traitor's stead, the Table would crack and Death itself would start working backward." [6](The Lion, the Witch and the Wardrobe 178-179)

Like Aslan's strategic death, Christ's sacrifice in the face of our Lawbreaking not only satisfies the demands written on Moses' tablets of stone, the Covenant of the Law, but it reverses the deathly consequences which that covenant carries for trespassers.

Lewis's elaborate metaphor breaks down here; for, it is not the Law which breaks at this point, but man himself: "For I through the Law died to the Law that I might live to God" (Galatians 2:19). Present in Christ when He expires upon the cross, man dies to the Law of sin and

---

6. C.S. Lewis, *The Lion, the Witch and the Wardrobe* (New York: HarperCollins, 1978), 178-79.

The Fortunate Fall

death. "I have been crucified with Christ; it is no longer I who live, but Christ lives in me, and the life which I now live in the flesh I live by faith in the Son of God, who loved me and gave Himself for me" (Galatians 2:20). Death is swallowed up in victory. New life comes, and it animates everything with the magical love that seeded it. Consequently, we can likewise say with Paul, "Thanks be to God, who delivers me through Jesus Christ our Lord!" (Romans 7:25).

If it is true that God uses even sin to accomplish His good purposes in our lives, we do not have to live in a state of paranoia that we will sin unwittingly. We have our hands full addressing the temptations and sins we do see in ourselves without ferreting out the sins hidden from our eyes because they are so deeply imbedded in our flesh. The Scriptures say that God makes the wrath of man to praise Him, suggesting that He makes all the wrathful sins of humanity to become a paean of praise to Him, His goodness, His mercy, and His ability to make all things new (Psalm 76:10). God is more than capable of saving us from our hidden sins. So, go ahead; live! As my optimistic husband encourages me, throw open the proverbial screen door each day, and do what your hand finds to do.

In the arena of homeschooling, I would bet that you are doing this already. Most of us do not set out to sin against our kids. In fact, we exert all our efforts in the opposite direction! Since they are the loves of our lives, sinning against our kids feels a lot like sinning against ourselves. As products of our one-flesh-relationships with our spouses, they are truly flesh of our flesh and bone of our bone (Genesis 2:23). In fact, I have spent much of my motherhood learning through my experiences that my kids are not actually an extension of me. That sounds silly, I know, but I think that, however intellectually we may concede that our kids are individuals, our hearts must learn this viscerally.

Consider that the child starts as a perceived part of the mother's self. In pregnancy, the very being of the child is nestled within her body. Separation starts immediately at birth, and the process continues for the length of the child's and the mother's lives. I'm not sure that it is ever fully accomplished for the mother, although healthy children do seem to manage it in time.

This biological phenomenon demonstrates the wisdom of God in planning for the propagation of the species, which is not only a physical miracle, but also a psychological one. In His wisdom, He saw the selfishness worked into human flesh and worked with it, rather than against it. If, He seemed to posit, they will think only of themselves, we will make sure they see their children as extensions of themselves. That way they will love each child like their own bodies, consider its things their own, and treasure it. Leave it to God to find a way to make the sinful selfishness and egocentrism He foresaw in humanity work for good in His plan to propagate the species! He truly does work all things together for good!

Of course, I do not mean to say that this is without pitfalls, but consider them. Even they have the makings of redemption within them. In the process of sinning against our children, we are stripped of our self-righteousness and directed to Jesus, the only source of justification. From this position, when we revisit the initial question (How do I avoid this?), we find the only logical response to be, "Why would you want to do that?"

Chapter 13

Blind Kings, Man-Eaters, and Getting What We Don't Deserve: Finding Life Through Death

> *"Mine eyes are not the best. I'll tell you straight."* [1]

In truth, the parent/child relationship is often the only relationship potent enough to provoke some of us to admit our hopeless condition. We avoid self-sight until it is absolutely necessary because it smacks of death – death of what ragamuffin theologian Brennan Manning calls "the imposter," the glittering image of self we so carefully erect for ourselves and others to admire: "The false self buys into outside experiences to furnish a personal source of meaning. The pursuit of money, power,

---

1. William Shakespeare, *King Lear* in *The Great Books of the Western World Vol. 25*, ed. Mortimer J. Adler et al. (Chicago: Encyclopaedia Britannica, 1990), 5.3.278.

glamour, sexual prowess, recognition, and status enhances one's self-importance and creates the illusion of success. The imposter is what he does...The imposter is a liar." [2] Our children have the potential to be the death of our self-glorification projects.

Since our kids have been with us since the time they were within us, we have grown used to them. Consequently, when we are with them, we are rarely pretending. They get the real us, unedited, which can be pretty scary stuff. We need not worry, though, because that reality goes both ways. We were there when little Johnny was pooping on himself. He, too, has been "seen." We know him – the good, the bad, and the ugly – just as he knows us. This mutual vulnerability, far from a liability, may be the greatest mercy God has ever shown to us. Understood properly, it has the potential to become the seedbed of deep and abiding relationship with our children.

This unique bond puts us all in the position of having to see ourselves as we are. Our primal relationships are at stake here; so, we might actually be willing to do what, for any lesser reason, we would not. Rarely are we willing to own our sins and to take responsibility for the debacles that plague our relationships. It feels like death, and we do a lot of blame-shifting to avoid it. We edit the narratives of our lives to justify ourselves and are all too willing to indict others to avoid the crushing guilt associated with self-recognition.

---

2. Brennan Manning, *Abba's Child: The Cry of the Heart for Intimate Belonging* (Colorado Springs: Navpress, 2002), 17.

Such is the case with William Shakespeare's foolish King Lear. Inflated with his sense of superiority, the aged Lear conceives of a plan that will divest him of responsibility for his kingdom without depriving him of his authority. To enact this self-interested plan, the egocentric ruler invents a game by which his daughters will perjure themselves in flattery of him. When his youngest and most cherished daughter refuses to play, he flies into a blind rage. This blindness persists despite the counsel of his most trusted advisor, who exhorts him to "check his hideous rashness:" [3] "See better, Lear; and let me still remain the true blank of thine eye." [4] Yet far from heeding this counsel, Lear stops his ears and closes his eyes. He rants, raves, and rages.

When evidence of his folly assaults him in the persons of his vicious and calculating elder daughters, who strip him of title, power, and honor, he takes shelter in, of all things, a horrific storm: "Thou thinkest 'tis much that this contentious storm/ invades us to the skin. So 'tis to thee;/ But where the greater malady is fix'd, the lesser is scarce felt…When the mind's free/ The body's delicate. The tempest in my mind/ Doth from my senses take all feeling else/ Save what beats there…" [5] Rather than face his own sin, Lear exposes himself to the elements and even the wrath of the gods, contending that he is "a man more sinned against than sinning." [6] Ar-

---

3. Shakespeare, *King Lear*, 1.1.152-52.
4. Ibid., 1.1.160-61.
5. Ibid., 3.4.6-14.
6. Ibid., 3.2.58-59.

gument can be made that this blame-shifting is the very source of his madness.

Yet, by the play's conclusion, the elements and their divine masters have done their good work upon him, and Lear begins to see. Captured by his enemy and imprisoned with his dear Cordelia, he finds himself the object of the machinations of Lord Gloucester's bastard son Edmund, who orders their executions. When Lear's faithful subjects discover the plot and race to free him, they find the guard dead and Lear cutting down Cordelia's corpse. He has summoned his old nobility, fighting to protect the daughter he wronged, but cherished.

Released from bondage and bearing Cordelia's body, Lear returns to the stage and greets his old advisor Kent with changed countenance, confessing: "Mine eyes are not the best. I'll tell you straight."[7] For Lear, this change comes too late. His reticence to see himself and forsake his own glittering image leads to the death of his children and war within his kingdom's borders. The final words of the play belong to the Duke of Albany, and they figuratively point to the play's thematic content: "We that are young shall never see so much, nor live so long."[8] Albany knows that Lear's experience with sin and its consequences gave him a vision of human depravity available only to the old. The epic scope of the aged king's blindness reaps epic consequences. In his brokenness, Lear presents a compelling vision of nobility, humbled by self-sight. Through him, Shakespeare

---

7. Shakespeare, *King Lear*, 5.3.278.
8. Ibid., 5.3.325-26.

prods his readers to consider the consequences of blind self-justification.

Most of us parents consider relationships with our children important enough that we are willing to do for our kids what we would not do even for ourselves. For them we might be willing to tell the truth, to tear down our glittering image, the tarnished mask we present to the world. To preserve our relationships with our children, we, too, might be willing to face our Golgotha.

This, incidentally, goes for Junior, too. A parent is one of the most important people in an individual's life. Psychologists take in billions a year for therapy sessions with people whose parental relationships slipped sideways. For our children, it is possible that a healthy relationship with Mom and Dad and the foundational validation and support it offers will drive him to deal with his own issues, too, but that is a different story. We have our hands full with our own.

So, there you stand, exposed, having violated in some way the lawful expectations of parenthood. The law stands in judgment of your behavior, and you have two choices: You can admit your sin, repent and seek reconciliation in forgiveness, or you can blameshift and demand your rights in the proceedings. According to Romans 6:23, these rights entitle us, ironically, to death: "The wages of sin is death." Since we all sin, we all deserve to die.

This verse suggests that the real choice is actually one between death and death (after all, no one gets out of this life thing alive); so, why not get on with the repugnant business and die here and now? Die to your right to be right, the million parts of the problem that were not your fault, and own the million parts that were. My mother-in-law used to ask me whenever I was "in a twit" about relationship problems, "Do you want to be right, or do you want to have a relationship?" By the grace and mercy of God, we parents will choose relationship with our children over self-justification and die to ourselves willingly.

C.S. Lewis, in his beautiful retelling of the Cupid Psyche myth *Till We Have Faces*, presents a similar dilemma to his readers. The main character, Orual, confronted with her ugliness, constructs a narrative to justify herself and veils her face to avoid being seen. Masked, she walks unknown among her people, sure that her true face will doom her leadership and approval ratings. When encounters with people who have seen through her disguise expose her, she despairs and likens herself to Ungit, the bloodthirsty pagan god of her people, who requires men as sacrifice. She sees that she too is an "eater of men," exacting their lifeblood to sustain her identity. Horrified by the identification, she determines to commit suicide: "I am Ungit. I will not be Ungit," she asserts. Poised upon the bank of a river, her feet and hands bound, she hears the voice of the real god, Cupid, whom she has falsely accused of stealing her sister. He tells her that attempts to eradicate her sin through suicide are futile. She must die before she dies: "'Do not do it,' said the god. 'You cannot escape Ungit by going to the deadlands, for she is there also. Die before you die.

There is no chance after.'"⁹

Die before you die. This is the hope of the believer. Like Orual, we parents are offered this chance to die to our self-constructed narratives of self-justification and to embrace the truth about ourselves. That is, as Lewis indicates, we are given the opportunity to discover our true faces. Like Orual, however, we often delay the process by our continued efforts at self-justification and blame-shifting. Orual's efforts to resolve her identity crisis disturb even her dreams:

> *It was a labour of sifting and sorting, separating motive from motive and both from pretext; and this same sorting went on every night in my dreams, but in a changed fashion. I thought I had before me a huge, hopeless pile of seeds, wheat, barley, poppy, rye, millet, what not? and I must sort them out and make separate piles, each all of one kind. Why I must do it, I did not know; but infinite punishment would fall upon me if I rested a moment from my labour or if, when all was done, a single seed were in the wrong pile. In waking life, a man would know the task impossible. The torment of the dream was that, there, it could conceivably be done...*¹⁰

Justification by the keeping of the law requires perfection, which is conceivable, but not achievable.

---

9. C.S. Lewis, *Till We Have Faces: A Myth Retold* (San Diego: Harcourt Brace & Co., 1980), 279.
10. Lewis, *Till We have Faces*, 256.

When Orual finally receives the audience she demands with the gods, she sees herself and her petty grievances clearly. She awaits judgment in penitent silence, her lovely, graceful sister, Psyche, the betrothed of Cupid, at her side:

> *The voices spoke again; but not loud this time. They were awed and trembled. "He is coming," they said. "The god is coming into his house. The god comes to judge Orual."*
>
> *If Psyche had not held me by the hand I should have sunk down. She had brought me now to the very edge of the pool. The air was growing brighter and brighter about us; as if something had set it on fire. Each breath I drew let into me new terror of joy, overpowering sweetness. I was pierced through and through with the arrows of it. I was being unmade. I was no one. But that's little to say; rather, Psyche herself was, in a manner, no one...it was not, not now, she that really counted. Or if she counted (and oh, gloriously she did) it was for another's sake. The earth and stars and sun, all that was or will be, existed for his sake. And he was coming. The most dreadful, the most beautiful, the only dread and beauty there is, was coming. The pillars on the far side of the pool flushed with his approach. I cast down my eyes.*
>
> *Two figures, reflections, their feet to Psyche's feet and mine, stood head downward in the water. But whose*

were they? Two Psyches, the one clothed, the other naked? Yes, both Psyches, both beautiful (if that mattered now) beyond all imagining, yet not exactly the same.

"You also are Psyche," came a great voice.[11]

We, too, are Psyche, beloved of the God of Love. Having seen ourselves and repented, we, like Orual, are poised for the joy of being truly justified, fully known, and fully loved by the God of grace. God's declarative love makes us beautiful and gives us a lasting identity.

Be honest. How many of you believe that you would still be loved if the Orual part of you that you keep veiled — you know, that selfish, man-devouring part of you that demands pre-eminence and service even at the expense of those you love — were suddenly made known to others? Do you not fear that, in such a case, you would experience rejection, loneliness, and despair? Do you not secretly believe that you are unacceptable? Is this not one of the reasons you work so hard to justify yourself – in order to be worthy of love and relationship? What if all of that were unnecessary? What if you were already in? What if you were, in fact, both fully known and fully loved? Would that change anything for you?

I have good news for you, and I never get tired of saying it because I so desperately need to hear it myself: You are fully known. God both sees and knows you. He sees through the public face you wear to the you under-

---

11. Lewis, *Till We Have Faces*, 308-309.

neath. He understands you better than you understand yourself. Full of pity and compassion, He saw you even before you were conceived and knew what you would need. "For he chose us in Him before the creation of the world to be holy and blameless in His sight. In love He predestined us for adoption to sonship through Jesus Christ, in accordance with His pleasure and will..." (Ephesians 1:4-5). In love and power, the Lord emptied Himself of His divinity and became incarnate in the person of Jesus Christ. He lived, perfectly keeping the Law of His Father God (and all of the "little-l" laws that emanate from it), and then He died the shameful death of a lawbreaker. His merit in life and death He credits to your account. This is the Gospel; this is the Good News.

How does the Gospel help the homeschool parent with the problems we have identified? What did Jesus's death upon that cross two thousand years ago accomplish for you and me? Well, to take up Lewis's myth once more, it gives us a face. Metaphorically speaking, we are no longer Ungit, the devourers of men. Instead we are Psyche, the bride of the God of Love. We have not been left to sort and count the seeds in the storeroom laboriously, as Orual was in her vision. It is not for us to earn our place through strict accounting and copious attention to detail. We have received help from the outside. We have been given a new and better identity, a spotless record that can never be taken from us. Since it comes to us on the basis of Jesus' perfection, it stands outside of the economy of earnings and losses, a credit to our account by grace. Far from the exchange of labor and wages, grace works by means of death and resurrection.

In my own story, while my initial reaction to Ian's confrontational words to my husband and me was one of self-justification, the seed-counting that followed in my own life exposed my real condition. Try as I did to sort things out into a case in my favor, the job proved too difficult. The Law was exacting; every seed must be in its place. The impossibility of this work drove me to abandon my defense. With my "stuff" lying around in piles, I was forced to seek a better justification. In the process, I found a new humility taking root which would lead me to empathize with my son. We had made a mess of things, the two of us. We had misconstrued everything, but the Lord makes the wrath of man to praise Him. As the preacher of Ecclesiastes declares, He makes everything beautiful in its time. The very seeds that littered my floor became the garden of our friendship.

This is the story which God has woven into the fabric of the universe; is it so strange that we should find it in the arena of family and homeschooling? Once we have eyes to see it, we find this paradigm everywhere: in Shakespeare's *King Lear*, in Lewis's *Till We Have Faces*, in Tolstoy's *War and Peace*, in Elizabeth George Speare's *The Bronze Bow*, in Gary Schmidt's *Orbiting Jupiter*, in Jane Austen's *Emma*, in Milton's *Paradise Lost*. From age to age, across continents and generations, authors are preoccupied with identity and grace. Death and resurrection shape the major story line of God's epic history of the world, and the themes it evinces are those of hope, redemption, love, relationship, and newness of life.

So, what do we do if we discover our inner Ungit at work in our best efforts with our children? We die – to ourselves, to our glittering image of perfection and performance, to our preconceived expectations and plans. We admit our frail creaturehood and model the fabric of the Christian experience – death and resurrection – in the form of repentance, seeking forgiveness and reconciliation with our children and God.

To our children, we can utter with Orual: "Never again will I call you mine; but all there is of me shall be yours. Alas, you know now what it's worth. I never wished you well, never had one selfless thought of you. I was a craver."[12] To our God, we can utter with Job: "My ears had heard of you but now my eyes have seen you. Therefore, I despise myself and repent in dust and ashes" (Job 42:5-6). From God, we know we have what we seek. He cannot deny Himself, and He atoned for those sins we confess so that we would belong to Him and never be alone. From our children, however, we must sometimes patiently wait to obtain forgiveness. Sinners, too, they must find their own faces before they have the grace to look on ours with love.

If your own story is still in process, don't despair! Our experience with God gives us hope. The same God who has loved us, loves them. If He has loved us enough to confront us with truth so that we would discover without our veils that we are both fully known and fully loved, then will He not faithfully do so for our children

---

12. Lewis, *Till We Have Faces*, 305.

also? And will not that self-knowledge breed an empathy, a camaraderie, a shared experience that makes us not only children and parents, but also fellow creatures, beloved children of God, and finally friends?

Our mutual depravity fosters a mutual need for grace. It levels the playing field and places us all right where we belong, at the foot of the cross. From that vantage, our sins atoned for even as those against us are validated, we begin to see that all that really matters is Christ crucified. Having looked upon Jesus's death, we stand with Thomas in the upper room, awaiting proof of His rumored resurrection. Like Thomas, we will not be disappointed. The Lord will manifest that resurrection, even as He manifested Himself to Thomas, in our relationships. He will discover us and cover us simultaneously, in an act of profound knowledge and compassion. He will restore and renew us for our tasks, furnishing us with companions for life's blind journey of faith.

So, go, seek out your kids, and repent. I did, and here's what happened: As I narrated the history of our broken relationship to my son, I realized that he had never heard it from me before. He was ignorant of the things the Lord had shown me regarding my sin. How could he have known what I didn't share with him? As I confessed my sin, he was quick to own his own. Each of us validated the other's experience, and grace began its good work. Mutual forgiveness set us both free from the bondage of our sins. No longer did we carry the shame of our failures. Instead our love for one another gave us both a new name – friend. Our relationship was more than restored; it was transformed. So do it; don't be afraid. The relationships that await you far surpass all your carefully laid plans. Homeschool in view of the gospel of grace. Delight in being home, a safe environment where you can learn together with your children that you are fully known and fully loved.

If it is only a day gone wrong that you are attempting to fix, count yourself blessed. Say that you are sorry and bake some cookies. If it is a year, repent and start again with your new self-knowledge fully in your sights. If on your way through this book you have discovered that you have done it all wrong, that your entire homeschooling career was fraught with performancism, and it is too late for a do-over – despair not!

Because we serve a living God, life always comes out of death. It may be too late to change your homeschool environment, but it is never too late to repent. The reeking compost of your homeschooling career may become the seed-bed of a new relationship with your children. My own relationship with my son was newly born the day I confessed my fault in our trouble. What is more, my acknowledgement of guilt communicated the genuine nature of my love and acceptance of him, and he was set free to see himself and to own his own sin in the matter. What once was a finger-pointing affair for us both has now become a mutual attempt to assume all the blame and exonerate the other. Our joint refrain has become, "It's all my fault!" When you see your own sins clearly, the sins of the other look small. And when you know you are loved, covering the other is joy.

Maybe you have not made the leap into homeschooling yet. You picked up this book contemplating the decision, and now you are not so sure. If homeschooling is such a loaded gun, why would anyone ever pick it up? Here is your answer: Life is a loaded gun. You cannot avoid it. If it is true that death and resurrection is the story God is telling in every life, then death will find you regardless of your own life's particulars. If you avoid it in homeschooling by throwing your kiddos into a day school, it will find you there in report cards, in the PTA, in the social scene. If it misses you in this arena, it will find you in your day job, in your friendships, in your homemaking efforts, in your marriage.

In our ceaseless attempts to justify ourselves, everything in our lives is fodder for fire. By avoiding homeschooling, we merely exchange one arena of grace for another, but know that grace will surely come. The goodness of God ensures it. His love for us promises it. His word spells it out:

> *We know that in everything God works for good with those who love him, who are called according to his purpose. For those whom he foreknew he also predestined to be conformed to the image of his Son, in order that he might be the first-born among many brethren. And those whom he predestined he also called; and those whom he called he also justified; and those whom he justified he also glorified.* (Romans 8:28-30)

We cannot outrun the probing searchlight of God. Like

Abraham, we must take Him as He is: a smoking oven and a burning torch. He will shine the light of that torch into the hidden recesses of our hearts and illuminate all that lies within, and He will burn up the filth He finds there with His passionate love, leaving us clean and pure.

While the process of coming to know ourself is painful, it is a severe mercy. As Lewis suggests in another one of his classic works, *The Great Divorce*: "If you would drink the cup of shame, you would find it very nourishing..." For we were made to worship God, and until our self is dethroned, we will never know the joy of doing that for which we were born, never experience the rest to which we have been called.

Chapter 14

Graceful Homeschooling

> "We could thus also say that Socrates is one who is truly in billions, the most powerful confirmation that we have of what is, after all, not merely an individual but a generally human possibility – the mind's ability to behold and consider itself and its works." [1]

Because of the gospel of grace, we no longer lack a "face." We have an identity, hidden with Christ in God. In the absence of this need to create ourselves, our teaching efforts can become what they were always meant to be: activities. Rather than a means to success or identity, our work with our children can become a product of our loving relationship with God.

Moreover, because God is not evaluating our performance to determine our merit, we can relax and enjoy the tasks He has put before us. How well we do them

---

1. Richard Mitchell, *The Gift of Fire*, 22.

Graceful Homeschooling

will in no way affect our standing with Him, in no way erode our identity as beloved children. Neither our successful performance nor our abject failure can justify us before God. We are justified freely by His grace. We are the ones that Jesus loves, and nothing can rob the believing heart of His good favor.

Think of what a game changer this could be in your practical role as a homeschooling mom! Suddenly, with the threat of failure removed from the table, you can acknowledge your shortcomings and begin the arduous task of addressing them. Likewise, since you no longer depend upon your children's performance for validation, you are free to acknowledge their shortfall, too. The environment of acceptance and honesty that the gospel of grace cultivates is imperative for learning to occur. Where there is fear of failure and rejection, the learning process is still-born, thwarted by hiding, posturing, and pride; but where there is grace, there is humility, the necessary precondition for learning.

When a mother believes that her identity is in her work with her children, they become the measure of her success. When her children succeed in their schooling and behave well, she considers herself a winner. When they fail at their work and struggle in their development, she considers herself a loser. The degree of pressure that this places on the parent-child relationship is unreasonable.

Children were not born to validate their parents. In fact, in the parent-child relationship, it is the parent who rightly ought to serve the child, and not the other way around. In as much as parents represent the image of God (however marred) in their relationship with their children, they are called to, like Him, lay down their lives – to die so that their children can live. Parents rightly fulfill the suffering servant's role in the family drama, and not their kids.

Having seen the original Suffering Servant and benefited from the validation He procured, we Christian parents are poised and ready to follow in His footsteps, laying down our lives so that our people can live. Rather than using the stuff of our lives to save ourselves, we are free to lose ourselves for the sake of our children. We can spend ourselves on their behalf because our success has already been secured by Jesus' work on our behalf.

With our "selves" out of the way, we are free to teach. Having gained for ourselves a real education, we are prepared to begin educating our children. How are we to lead our children into growing self-knowledge? Is there a particular educational paradigm that best serves this purpose?

I would wager that all methodologies are useful tools when utilized with this greater goal in view. Consider: Mastery Learning techniques reveal the abilities and weaknesses of the child, demonstrating both his grandeur and misery. In his success, he images the Lord. In his failures, he finds his humanity. Delight Directed Learning reveals the child's inborn preferences; the child discovers the unique personality the Lord created in him. Classical, Socratic discussions help the child question the world and his place within it; exercises in rhet-

Graceful Homeschooling

oric force him to watch himself think, a process which often reveals the unexamined assumptions and sloppy logic natural to fallen creatures.

Regardless of the pedagogical techniques you prefer in the classroom, a focus on using them to confront childish egocentrism and uncover the reality of the student's condition will undoubtedly prove fruitful. Grades pale in significance, except for the opportunity they render in service of this ideal.

In addition, if mastery isn't the ultimate goal of education, coverage ceases to become the ultimatum of class business, the dictator of time. Suddenly, we are free to take advantage of "teachable moments," those significant opportunities that occur when sleeping students begin to stretch and yawn, and the fog begins to clear. Questions form like arrows on their lips, shafts of revelation that cause stunned silence, profound wonder, deep introspection, sorrow, or joy.

Richard Mitchell notes such a moment in *The Gift of Fire*:

> So now I can see before me one of those persons whom I call, in a very strange manner of speaking, 'my' students. There she sits, as close to the back of the classroom as possible. She is blowing bubbles with her gum, and not without skill. She intends to be a schoolteacher...Someday, perhaps this day, when I have explained some difficult proposition's exploration by Emerson, that young woman...will raise her hand and ask the question, and ask it just as Socrates asked, out of what

> *she knows to be her ignorance, and her desire not to be ignorant. And her question will remind me that I am ignorant, and that I didn't know it, and that I do not want to be...and in that moment, in the world that then and there exists, who is the teacher and who the student? Who is Socrates? ...And in that moment when she is Socrates I may well be seeing the first moment of thoughtfulness in her life. Education, real education, and not just the elaborate contraption that is better understood as 'schooling,' can be nothing but the nourishment of such moments.*[2]

Making room for these moments is the role of a good teacher; this is the role of a good parent; this is the role of a good friend. And when these moments occur, taking the position of student alongside our children, remembering our own want and wonder, and searching out answers together is often all that is needed.

How different this is from the popular sketch of the Master Teacher, the answer man who knows it all and can dispel any question! If we were to return to Socrates, that famous thinker and profoundly wise man, we would discover that the secret to his success was not his mastery of knowledge, but his confession of ignorance. If this confession be wisdom — this learning, then all men have the potential to be Socrates: "We could thus also say that Socrates is one who is truly in billions, the most powerful confirmation that we have of what is, after all,

---

2. Richard Mitchell, *The Gift of Fire*, 21-22.

not merely an individual but a generally human possibility – the mind's ability to behold and consider itself and its works."[3] Ignorance is what all men have in common. Those billions who recognize and live from this truth are wise in the Socratic sense.

From the position of creaturehood, the world and everything in it beckons us to explore. Add to this the Christian truth that we are all known and loved, and the world becomes our stomping ground, a place made for us, full of truth and goodness, beauty and grace. Grace and its Author, this is the end of education. This is success. This is joy. This is life. To find this is everything. To give it to our children is to give them the world.

---

3. Richard Mitchell, The Gift of Fire, 22.

Chapter 15

Things I Would Tell My Younger Self

> "My crown is in my heart, not on my head;
> Not decked with diamonds and Indian stones,
> Nor to be seen. My crown is called content—
> A crown it is that seldom kings enjoy." [1]

What does this educational philosophy mean in the daily homeschooling experience? First, it means that it is not about the grade, for us or for our children. It means that we can abort the quest for perfection, ours and theirs, and begin a new journey together to discover the joys of our creaturehood. Like Shakespeare's good and gentle King Henry VI, we can discover the beauty and the benefits of being not a king, but a subject.

In Shakespeare's play, Henry's right to the throne has

---

1. William Shakespeare, *The Third Part of King Henry the Sixth* in *The Great Books of the Western World Vol. 24,*. ed. Mortimer J. Adler et al. (Chicago: Encyclopaedia Britannica, 1990), 3.1.62-65.

been challenged, and he is hounded and hassled to the point of despair. Having fled the throne, he casts off his tenuous crown and laments, "Was never subject long'd to be a king/ As I do long and wish to be a subject."[2] Like his grandfather before him, Henry affirms, "Uneasy the head that wears the crown." A King's power is ever threatened; anxiety is his constant companion.

Similarly, the crown of self-sovereignty we chase through performance is elusive and dangerous at best. Better by far is the lot of the subject, whose identity and portion is maintained by the true King. When we see Him, we can lay down our constantly receding hopes of attaining position through our achievements and receive instead the hope of Christ, the true inheritance of the Kingdom. When questioned by the world regarding our identity as recipients of this bequest, we can reply with Henry: "My crown is in my heart, not on my head;/ Not decked with diamonds and Indian stones,/ Nor to be seen. My crown is called content— / A crown it is that seldom kings enjoy."

Practically speaking, for homeschoolers this means that we can make study, rather than mastery, the goal of our daily efforts. We can spend time pondering the nature of things and delight in the discovery of our smallness in this large world. Freed from the need to master all things, we can investigate what it means to be creatures. In the process, we can lay aside the tyrannous demands of the booklist and the pressing expectations of

---

2. Ibid., 4.9.5-6.

the curriculum to simply look at one another.

For the homeschool mother of preschool and elementary children, this means that, when a homeschool day just isn't happening, it is okay to put the books away and bake cookies! We can cancel desk work and go for a hike, play in the yard, or gather everyone on the sofa for reading time. We can pick up the living room or address the looming pile of laundry in the corner. We can be at home with ourselves and our children.

For the parent of junior high kids, it means that we can embrace the frivolity, the temporary giddiness of our children's youth, without undue fear for their future. We can watch movies, play games, and enter their social world without condemnation. We can alternate between deep and meaningful discussions of the transcendentals and conversations about their latest favorite pop stars. The earth is the Lord's, and so are they.

For parents of high schoolers, it means that we can face the pressures of college prep and entrance exams without serving them as idols. We can enjoy the pursuit of knowledge and wisdom for their own sake, rather than for the meaty scholarships they might yield or the stamp of validation a third-party institution accrues. We can follow and respond to the interests of our kids and help them discover their unique creaturehood, the design worked into their lives, unearthing their gifts and calling, even if that calling may be one the world will never regard. Whereas the paradigm of identity through activity demands notable careers and measurable success, identity through Christ sets us free to live and to serve in anonymity if we are so called.

What if your homeschool project has been derailed by rebellious kids? Knowledge of our secure identity in Christ allows us to embrace the suffering, knowing that, ultimately, suffering does not mean failure. Our children's difficulties are painful enough when we experience them vicariously without all the self-flagellation a retributive paradigm produces. By the economy of grace, we can look through the suffering toward the hope of Christ, knowing that He tears down to rebuild (Zechariah 1:18-21). The present appearance of failure is not the final word on the subject because you and your child are not all there is. God is, and with Him is mercy. True to His nature, He faithfully keeps His promises and will "perfect that which concerns [you]" (Psalm 138:8).

If I had to guess, I'd bet you opened this book looking for some how-to lists. I like lists myself, but in the case of this book, I've hoped to give you something better. I'd like to give you freedom and rest! In that spirit and in view of my experience homeschooling over the past 25 years, I have made a list of **Things I Wish I Could Tell My Younger Self**.

📖

1.) Homeschooling is about home, and home is about family. The family is the central and singular aspect of the homeschool experience. Remember your relationships. No subject you study, curriculum you complete (or fail to complete), grades you assign, or project you accomplish is more important to the education you are providing your children than this. Try as you may to create a classroom in your home, it remains a home. Be at home. Be a family. Be a mom. In the end, it is your best bet, your greatest asset, and the last hat remaining when the monolithic schooling project is done.

2.) Relax. The curriculum is not your god. Completing it does not represent successful education any more than failing to complete it represents a lack of it. It is just curriculum, just a tool by which to practice the art of learning. If it is good curriculum, it will guide you in your exploration of the permanent things. Major in these.

3.) Technical mastery is not the final goal of a liberal arts education. Consider the student who took a degree in early computer programming and learned assembly language, now virtually obsolete. Or imagine the student who took a college degree in the steam engine, only to find his degree worthless when the combustion engine hit the scene. Instead of working toward a technical education, teach kids *how* to learn. Give them the tools to pursue any subject, and they will be equipped for a lifetime of re-inventing themselves.

4.) Remember that there is a difference between cultural literacy and education. While cultural literacy is important and requires some knowledge of subject matter, education (as my professor suggested to me with his extremely short booklist) may be achieved with a single book! The process of education has more to do with equipping individuals with what Dorothy Sayers called the "tools of learning."[3] Children taught how to "watch themselves think" will be prepared to spend a lifetime thinking and learning about the world and their place in it.

5.) Stop worrying about what other people think! It is a waste of your time. Besides, most of the time, they are not thinking about you. They are too busy worrying and thinking about themselves to bother with you at all! Be yourself.

6.) No one expects your home to look like a magazine but you. Not only that, but the magazines are sets, not real places where people actually live. When I was a kid, my best friend had a father who wanted his home to look like a museum. Neither of us liked to be there, even though it was lovely. We preferred to be someplace we could sit down or use the kitchen. Your house is a home where people live, and that means some mess. Go to the museum for a day trip or enjoy the beauty of a magazine, but live at home. You and your family will be much more comfortable.

---

3. Classical educator and author Dorothy Sayers' essay, "The Lost Tools of Learning," argues that education is less the learning of specific bodies of information and more the acquisition of how to learn. She delineates the stages of human development and suggests useful teaching tools appropriate to each stage.

7.) Repent! Out loud! To your kids! Admit your wrongdoing, and you will be giving them permission to admit their own. Please model repentance to your children. It is the most important thing you will ever teach them. Remember that the ability to confess sin and repent is the earmark of Christianity, evidence of membership in God's family.

First John tells us that, "when we walk in the light as He is in the light, we have fellowship with one another and the blood of Christ Jesus cleanses us from every sin." My father-in-law, a preacher, elucidates this verse with a grammar exercise: He observes that the verse follows the same grammatical structure as that in the following sentence: If you can read the bottom line of the eye chart, then your vision is 20/20. Consider that reading the bottom line of the eye chart does not give you 20/20 vision, but only demonstrates that you possess it. Likewise, our confession of sin does not earn us forgiveness, but rather evidences that we have been forgiven. Only believers are truly capable of admitting their sin. Confession is a gift from God that evidences His merciful forgiveness and justification. With this guarantee of forgiveness, you are free to tell the truth about yourself. Furthermore, knowledge that God has forgiven you makes it possible to forgive yourself and others. When we walk in repentance, we teach our children that perfection is not required for relationship, that a Christian is rather one who repents and looks to Christ for righteousness. So repent. Forgive yourself. Forgive your kids. Live gracefully.

8.) Encourage your kids with positive affirmation. Give them honor in your home as masterpieces of God and holy partakers of His goodness. Remind them that they are not what they do. Tell them that their identity has been secured from a time before they were ever born. (Ephesians 1:4) Bless them with your tongue even as you correct them. Tell them they are blessings to you and to others and watch them own this identity.

9.) Talk about the gospel continually. Look for grace in everything. Honor the last, the little, and the least, and identify with them in your own need.

10.) Delight yourself in the stuff of life. You are a creature, and the world is yours to enjoy. Take time to wonder. Cultivate the arts in your home. Sure, there is time! There is no hurry, since the goal is not completion. Take the time to create and enjoy beauty.

11.) Human beings are not just minds or disembodied spirits, but bodies too. Take time to exercise and to eat good food. The work will wait!

12.) Human beings need fellowship. Make time to cultivate friendships both inside and outside of the family. We were not meant to live alone with only our books for companions.

13.) Work and achievements are not the end goal of life, but the enjoyment of our identity in Christ. Be not driven. He has accomplished all things for you and for your children. Enter into His rest. Rest.

14.) Be compassionate with yourself and with others. After all, you are only dust. Live in light of your temporality.

> *Vanity of vanities, saith the Preacher, vanity of vanities; all is vanity. What profit hath a man of all his labour which he taketh under the sun? One generation passeth away, and another generation cometh: but the earth abideth for ever. The sun also ariseth, and the sun goeth down, and hasteth to his place where he arose. The wind goeth toward the south, and turneth about unto the north; it whirleth about continually, and the wind returneth again according to his circuits. All the rivers run into the sea; yet the sea is not full; unto the place from whence the rivers come, thither they return again. All things are full of labour; man cannot utter it: the eye is not satisfied with seeing, nor the ear filled with hearing. The thing that hath been, it is that which shall be; and that which is done is that which shall be done: and there is no new thing under the sun. Is there anything whereof it may be said, See, this is new? It hath been already of old time, which was before us.*
> (Ecclesiastes 1:2-10)

In all of your experience under the sun, embrace this

creaturehood; for it is a given. "There is nothing better for a man, than that he should eat and drink, and that he should make his soul enjoy good in his labour. This also I saw, that it was from the hand of God" (Ecclesiastes 2:24).

Life is a gift, not a race. Receive it and rejoice.

Afterword

"He who calls you is faithful, who also will do it."
(1 Thessalonians 5:24).

Lest anyone should mistake me, I feel a need to clarify a few things here at the end.

I would like to say that because of my failures, I am a better person. I would like to say that, since my revelation, I never use my work to establish my identity, never treat my kids like a way to establish my value. I would like to say that I approach each day of teaching from a conscious position of rest, relaxed and confident. I would like to present myself as one further down the road to holiness than the rest of the pack.

Of course, that would be lying. In truth, I find myself back in the same, familiar rat race pretty frequently. Left to my own devices, I turn from the glorious message of the gospel, from the identity secured for me by Christ Jesus, and take up my chisel to continue construction on the Image of Me. I hide behind masks, hoping others will not notice how thin they really are. I stew in shame for all that I think I am supposed to be.

Afterword

I still fret over my children's performance, worry about their futures, wonder if I have done enough, if I am enough. I still worry about "gaps" and stress over completing the curriculum. I still compare myself with others who have different gifts and feel less for it. When I am honest, I see that, both personally and professionally, I have not "progressed" beyond my basic gospel neediness.

I know, however, that He who has begun a good work in me will complete it until the day of Christ Jesus (Philippians 1:6). I know that, in the quest for righteousness and holiness, no believer is further along than I, nor I further along than any other believer. All believers possess the righteousness and holiness of Christ Jesus by imputation. How can one be any holier than that? I stand complete in Him.

Simultaneously saint and sinner, I am free to admit my defects – to announce them even! This honesty will constantly direct me (and any onlookers who might be tempted to comparison) back to the Source of all we need. Life, love, hope, help – Jesus has it all in His own person. Better still, He secured it and me when He fulfilled the terms of the Old Covenant. I enjoy a New Deal, better than the old because it cannot be made void, cannot be broken. God, the Executor, fulfilled all its terms when He took me with Him up onto the cross and expired in triumph, proclaiming it finished. (John 19:30)

That finished work of Christ is all I need; it is all we need. Though in this life we will vacillate between the Old Man and the New, we can expect to find ourselves resting from our crazed attempts to fix ourselves and trusting in Jesus' sufficient work more and more. We can expect to find ourselves admitting our sins and failures more readily, repenting to others more frequently.

Likewise, as we walk in this trust and repentance, we can expect to discover the fruits of the Holy Spirit growing out of our lives and endeavors. We can anticipate a new energy and desire to do the good works that "God has prepared beforehand for us to walk in" (Ephesians 2:10). We can expect the grace which has captivated us to permeate our lives and redeem our relationships. "He who calls you is faithful, who also will do it" (1 Thessalonians 5:24). Our only task is to look upon Him who was crucified, the reality of Moses' snake on the stick, Jesus. God made Him, who knew no sin, to be sin for us, so that in Him, we might become the righteousness of God (2 Corinthians 5:21). His grace is sufficient.

Bibliography

Alighieri, Dante. *The Divine Comedy.* Translated by Charles S. Singleton. *Great Books of the Western World.* Edited by Mortimer J. Adler. Chicago: Encyclopaedia Britannica,1990. 1-133.

Andrews, Robert. *The Scandalous Gospel of the Grace of God.* NY: Sentinel Press, 2011.

Augustine, Aurelius. *Confessions.* Edited by Albert C. Outler, Ph.D., D.D. U of Penn Linguistics Dept. www.ling.upenn.edu/courses/hum100/augustinconf.pdf. Accessed 4 October 2017.

—— *Enchiridion on Faith, Hope, and Love.* Edited by Albert C. Outler, Ph.D., D.D. Perkins School of Theology, 1955. www.tertullian.org/fathers/augustine_enchiridion_02_trans.htm. Accessed 31 Oct. 2017.

Austen, Jane. *Emma. The Great Books of the Western World Vol. 46.* Edited by Mortimer J. Adler et al. Chicago: Encyclopaedia Britannica, 1990. 3-197.

Brown, Steve. *Hidden Agendas [Dropping the Masks That Keep Us Apart].* Greensboro, NC: New Growth Press, 2016.

Calvin, John. *Institutes of the Christian Religion: 6th American Edition, Revised and Corrected, Volume 1.* Translated by John Allen. Philadelphia: Presbyterian Board of Publication, 1813. http://www.gutenberg.org/files/45001/45001-h/45001-h.html. Accessed 15 November 2017.

Capon, Robert Farrar. *Kingdom, Grace, Judgment: Paradox, Outrage, and Vindication in the Parables of Jesus*. Grand Rapids, MI: Eerdmans, 2002.

Condon, Sarah. *Churchy: The Real-Life Adventures of a Wife, Mom, and Priest*. Charlottesville, NC: Mockingbird Ministries, 2016.

Dostoevsky, Fyodor. *The Brothers Karamazov. The Great Books of the Western World Vol. 48*. Edited by Mortimer J. Adler et al. Chicago: Encyclopaedia Britannica, 1990.

Forde, Gerhard O. *On Being a Theologian of the Cross*. Grand Rapids, MI: Eerdmans, 1997.

Harris, Gregg. *The Christian Homeschool*. Salmon Creek, WA: Noble Publishing Associates, 1988.

Henley, William Ernest. "Invictus." 1875. *The Harp and the Laurel Wreath*. Edited by Laura M. Berquist. San Francisco: Ignatius Press, 1999.

Hirsch, E.D., Jr. "What Your ---- Grader Needs to Know." *The Core Knowledge Series*. NY: Bantam Books, 2014.

Lannon, Nick. "The Fosbury Flop (and the High Bar of the Law)." NickLannon.com www.nicklannon.com/2012/10/the-fosbury-flop-and-high-bar-of-law.

Bibliography

html. Accessed 9 October 2017.

Lewis, C. S. *The Great Divorce*. San Francisco, CA: HarperCollins Pub., 2001.

——— *The Lion, the Witch and the Wardrobe*. New York, NY: HarperCollins Pub., 1978.

——— *Till We Have Faces: A Myth Retold*. San Diego, CA: Harcourt Brace & Co., 1980.

Luther, Martin. *The Large Catechism*. Translated by F. Bente and W. H. T. Dau. St. Louis: Concordia Publishing House, 1921. http://www.gutenberg.org/cache/epub/1722/pg1722-images.html. Accessed 15 November 2017.

——— "Preface to Romans" from *Lectures on Romans*. messiah'skingdom.com, www.messiahskingdom.com/resources/The-Gospel/luther-romans.pdf. Accessed 4 October 2017.

Manning, Brennan. *Abba's Child: The Cry of the Heart for Intimate Belonging*. Colorado Springs, CO: Navpress, 2002.

Melville, Herman. *Moby Dick; or, The Whale*. *The Great Books of the Western World Vol. 48*. Edited by Mortimer J. Adler et al. Chicago: Encyclopaedia Britannica, 1990.

Milton, John. *Paradise Lost*. *The Great Books of the Western World Vol. 29*. Chicago: Encyclopaedia Britannica, 1990. 93-333.

Mitchell, Richard. *The Gift of Fire*. New York, NY: Simon & Schuster, Inc., 1987.

Moore, Raymond and Dorothy. *Better Late Than Early*. NY: Reader's Digest Association, 1989.

The New Open Bible. The New King James Version, 1st edition. Nashville, TN, 1990.

O'Connor, Flannery. *The Complete Stories*. NY: Farrar, Straus and Giroux, 1971.

—— "The Artificial Nigger." *The Complete Stories*. 249-270.

——"A Good Man Is Hard to Find." *The Complete Stories*. 117-133.

——"Revelation." *The Complete Stories*. 488-509.

Plato, *The Apology*. Translated by Benjamin Jowett. November 3, 2008. www.gutenberg.org/files/1656/1656-h/1656-h.htm. Accessed: 15 November 2017.

Robinson, Marilynne. *Home*. New York, NY: Farrar, Strauss and Giroux, 2008.

Rollins, Cindy. *Mere Motherhood*: *Morning Times, Nursery Rhymes, and My Journey Toward Sanctification*. Concord, NC: The Circe Institute, 2016.

Sayers, Dorothy. "The Lost Tools of Learning." *The Lost Tools of Learning and the Mind of the Maker*. Oxford: Oxford City Press, 2010.

Bibliography

Shakespeare, William. *The Second Part of King Henry the Sixth*. The Great Books of the Western World Vol. 24. Edited by Mortimer J. Adler et al. Chicago: Encyclopaedia Britannica, 1990. 63.

—— *The Third Part of King Henry the Sixth*. The Great Books of the Western World Vol. 24. Edited by Mortimer J. Adler et al. Chicago: Encyclopaedia Britannica, 1990. 85.

—— *King Lear*. The Great Books of the Western World Vol. 25. Edited by Mortimer J. Adler et al. Chicago: Encyclopaedia Britannica, 1990. 244-283.

Tchividjian, Tullian. *One Way Love: Inexhaustible Grace for an Exhausted World*. Colorado Springs, CO: David C. Cook, 2013.

Veith, Gene Edward and Andrew Kern. *Classical Education: The Movement Sweeping America*. Washington, DC: Capital Research Center, 2001.

Williamson, G. I. *The Shorter Catechism. Volume 1*. Presbyterian and Reformed Publishing Co., 1970.

About the Author

Missy Andrews is co-director of the Center for Literary Education and a homeschooling mother of six. She is the author of T*eaching the Classics: A Socratic Method for Literary Education* and *Wild Bells: A Literary Advent.* Missy earned her BA in English from Hillsdale College and her MA in imaginative literature from Harrison Middleton University. She and her husband Adam live on a mountaintop in northeast Washington, where she collects children's books and reads and reads and reads.